The Night is Dark and I am Far From Home

by

Doug Howell

India Company 3rd Battalion 5th
Marines
Special Landing Force
Okinawa 1966

On November 13, 1982, at the dedication of the Vietnam Veteran's Memorial in Washington, D.C., I had a long discussion with my oldest brother regarding my experiences in Vietnam. It was the first time I had ever spoken in depth to anyone about them. At the end of the discussion he said to me that these are memories that while painful, need to be shared with the public. He told me to write my memories down as they came to me, in bits and pieces in sort of a "letters to home" format. He then said to me "I'll even give you a title for your book of letters. Call it: *The Night is Dark and I am Far From Home.*"

It's been a long time coming Dave, and the book isn't exactly what we originally discussed, but it is a story that I truly believe should be told. You were the first to hear of my inner struggles and your inspiration will never leave me.

To the only person who knew all of my secrets during my darkest years, this book of letters home is dedicated.

Robert David Howell
October 15, 1943 – June 14, 1994

"….but until you heal the wounds of your past, you will continue to bleed. You can bandage the bleeding with food, with alcohol, with drugs, with work, with cigarettes, with sex, but eventually, it will all ooze through and stain your life. You must find the strength to open the wounds, stick your hands inside, pull out the core of the pain that is holding you in your past, the memories, and make peace with them."

Lyanla Vanzant, "Yesterday, I cried"

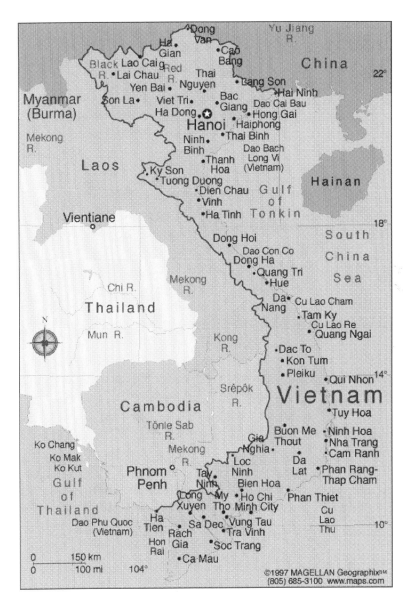

(*map from:* www.maps.com)

A trip forward into the past
Part One
April 25-May 10, 2008

Introduction

June 1, 2008

42 years ago, on a hill top nearly 10,000 miles from home, a group of U.S. Marines engaged in a ferocious fight. Ragged, with clothes literally falling off them, extremely low on ammunition, with no food and very little water, the members of India Company, 3rd Battalion 5th Marines, (I 3/5), hacked their way through the dense jungle near the eastern border of Laos and the North Vietnam border, along the DMZ, or Demilitarized Zone, northwest of Dong Ha.

The Marines had just survived an ambush by elements of the 324B Division of the North Vietnamese Army two nights previously in a stream bed near the Cam Lo River, close to mountain formations called The Rockpile and Razorback Ridge. They lost 13 men in that ambush, all from their 3rd platoon.

Hoping for resupply of much needed food, water and ammunition, they were told they had one more objective to carry out. The assignment seemed simple enough: erect and guard a "292" (tall) transmission antenna on a remote jungle hill top for better information relay in this rugged mountain area, and maintain its security.

The DMZ, which lay along the 17th parallel, was a no fire zone and technically there should have been no troop movement through this area. American reconnaissance showed, however, that the North Vietnamese Regular

Army (NVA) was amassing a huge force very close to this zone. The question was: Why?

Some U.S. Marine commanders thought the reason was to lure security troops away from the centers of Hue and DaNang so that they could attack these areas. The United States Army's General Westmoreland however did not agree with that assessment and very much wanted to go after this large group and stop them in their tracks before they made their way farther south toward Saigon, which is what he thought was their primary objective.

Since Westmoreland was the senior military commander of the Vietnam engagement, he made the decision to go after these NVA troops, and with that decision Operation Hastings was born. This operation was to become the largest U.S. Marine Corps operation in Vietnam to date. It proved to be one of the deadliest.

The Marines of India Company had made their way through the jungle to the base of their objective, Hill 362, at the far eastern end of what the American's called Mutter's Ridge. They spent a tense night guarding the dead and wounded from the stream bed ambush, knowing that there were large concentrations of enemy troops nearby. The next morning they asked for artillery support to "soften" hill 362 before assaulting it. It was hill 362 where the antenna was to be erected. This type of artillery support is commonly done to disperse or destroy any concentrations of enemy troops.

Unknown to the Americans, the NVA were already on the hill and their commanders, being excellent students of war, made a simple but brilliant counter move. After the first of the 105mm artillery shells hit the mountain, testing for accuracy, and before the Marines could give the order to "fire for effect," the NVA launched a single 82 mm mortar to the Americans flank. The Marines, always aware of the massive arsenal of the U.S., and cautious about casualties from "friendly fire," assumed that explosion on their left flank was a "short" artillery round from the supporting 105 mm cannons and ordered the shelling to stop. The NVA ploy worked perfectly. The hill was not softened up, and the Marines began pushing their way to the top. The NVA now had ample opportunity to set a deadly trap for this Marine company.

The Marines were approaching from the southwest. The topography of the hill was such that as you go over the top there is a saddleback or depression before once again going up a short way and then back down again on the northeast side.

The NVA positioned themselves east of the saddleback, with riflemen on one side of the trail, 12.8 mm (heavy) machine guns at the top of the second crest and 82mm mortars just beyond that, already aimed in on the trail. This position gave the NVA superior elevation along with their superior fire power. They outnumbered the Marines by at least 2:1, some reports had it at 3:1. We will never know the actual numbers. The Americans appeared to be walking straight into this trap.

India Company's first platoon had the point on the morning of July 24, 1966. They were not happy about the interrupted shelling of the hill. That should have been SOP (standard operating procedure). Over the past week, entire regimental and divisional NVA campgrounds and supplies had been discovered in the area; including an NVA hospital, engineering supplies and multiple caches of weapons. Reconnaissance was correct; the place was teeming with North Vietnamese soldiers. But these were

United States Marines and up the jungle mountain they went, hacking and slashing their way through the very dense underbrush. This was steep, triple canopy jungle mountain terrain and it was impossible to maneuver quietly.

Finally nearing the ridge line, they discovered a trail and a deserted enemy LP (listening post), with several lines of communication wire running up and down the trail. The trail ran up hill to the right and downhill to the left in a Northeast/Southwest fashion. Just then, four NVA soldiers came walking around the trail below them headed for the hill top. Very relaxed, they were carrying mortar rounds. When they spotted the Marines, they dropped their load and started running. Two were shot and killed, two were captured. One of the NVA soldiers indicated that there were many other soldiers on the hill but translation was iffy at best and the Marines could not determine whether the enemy was up the trail or down.

A brief meeting of officers at the point where they found the trail ensued. Some wanted more artillery on the hill. The CO (Company Commander) disagreed. One thing was for sure, the Marines were no longer in doubt of a coming fight.

Hoping to outflank the enemy, the first platoon leader, 2nd Lt. Sam Williams, thought the best chance of engagement was down the trail to the left and took his platoon in that direction. The second platoon now took point on the trail heading east up the hill, and took off in a hurry with the Command Group close behind. The third platoon, depleted from the ambush two nights previously, had finally evacuated its casualties and was still making its way up the hill. As the second platoon crested the hill and walked down into the saddle back, the NVA sprang the trap.

Chapter 1
War

June 2, 2008

It is difficult for most people who have not participated in war to understand men killing each other. In civilized society, the taking of another life is murder, legally defined and considered aberrant behavior. The notion "Thou shall not kill" permeates nearly every civilized culture and creed. In war however, the taking of life is expected and sanctified, and the side that is better at doing it is often the winner.

Training young, passionate, ground combat warriors to kill the enemies of their country is a more delicate process than you might imagine, the psychology of which is relieving these warriors of the very heavy burden of that killing. To do that, one must dehumanize the enemy, making him nothing more than a pest or rodent that needs to be eliminated. Once you understand the psychology of that, it becomes easier to understand some of the atrocities that occur. The desecration of the bodies of enemy soldiers is as old a practice as war itself, however unseemly to the lay public. War is a nasty and horrible business and certainly not for the weak of heart.

Just as tricky as facilitating the transition from innocence to warrior, is the transition back again, as the warrior has to fit back into civilized life. Getting back over that very dark and troubling line and figuring out how to deal with each individuals various level of success or failure at the original goal of killing, is fraught with psychological booby traps which haunt many war survivors for most if not all of their lives. Some never make it back across that line. Some never try.

Response to the frightening reality of the fighting itself however, is another matter and no one knows how they will respond in the pitch of battle, but with adequate training a certain level of discipline can be maintained even when there is chaos all around. This discipline begins in boot camp and continues until you find yourself in hostile territory either defending yourself or attacking your enemy, an enemy that is shooting back at you. It is this discipline that often makes the difference between survival and death.

Prior to Operation Hastings, India Company had been involved in many skirmishes and fire fights. The men were used to attacks from villages or hamlets or from the many tree lines that broke up the wide expanses of rice paddies. American Marine Corps units learned very quickly what the advantages of their enemy were: Concealment, territory familiarity and guerilla tactics. They also learned just as fast that fire discipline, accuracy and aggressiveness more than adequately compensated. Certainly these Marines were no strangers to fire fights and warfare, but none of those previous fights could compare to what was about to happen on that hill and how their mettle was going to be tested.

The 812th Regiment from the 324B Division of the North Vietnamese Army, numbering somewhere between 400 to 600 men, opened a withering barrage of fire on the second platoon, with their machine guns aimed straight down the trail, other NVA soldiers lying along the right flank of the trail for perpendicular fire, still others with 57mm recoilless rifles, and mortar teams poised to begin their own rain of terror.

Almost instantly, there were dead Marines all over the trail and the NVA mortars then began their deadly march over the crest of the first hill. The 1st platoon, sweeping down to the left had not yet made contact with the enemy and the sudden roar of the firefight above had them wheeling around to advance up the hill in support of the 2nd platoon, with the 3rd platoon now close behind the 1st, all of them double timing through a hail of mortars and gunfire to get to the site of action. In a very short time, nearly the entire company of some 200 men ran over the crest of that hill down into the depression. Little did they know that 48 hours later, only 63 would walk off.

Realizing that continuing down into the saddle back and up the other side was sure death, the Marines began to pull back to the top of the hill bringing their dead and wounded with them, but because of the density of the jungle growth, the intense cacophony of the fire fight, and the amount of grenades, small arms and mortar rounds expended, causing leaves, branches and all sorts of debris to fall from the jungle foliage, contributing to the ensuing chaos, it was impossible to tell if all the troops were accounted for. 1st platoon's Mike Bednar, who was the platoon radioman, along with George Corey and Frank Eucker, were just off the trail still defending their position among the many already dead and seriously wounded Marines. As the NVA realized the Marines were pulling back, they began to rush the ambush site, temporarily breaking through the Marines lines and overwhelming George, Mike and Frank. George was shot several times and died quickly. Mike and Frank had been critically wounded. Mike suffered a gunshot wound to the abdomen that exposed a large segment of his intestines. Knowing that they were being overrun and having no more ammunition, Mike and Frank lay as quietly as possible. Frank began moaning in pain from the number of bullet wounds he received and although he tried to stop when Mike told him to shut up, he could not help himself. An NVA soldier bayoneted him and he groaned. He was then shot in the head, execution style. Franklin C. Eucker, from East Orange, New Jersey was dead. He was 18 years old and he was my best friend.

Mike Bednar's stomach wounds were so gross that the enemy soldiers laughed and made comments about it. They took his watch, his pistol, his radio, his pack and his cigarettes. It was then his turn to be bayoneted and shot again. Only a remarkable thing happened. He did not make a sound when they put the bayonet into him and the shot missed him completely. Assuming he was dead, the NVA soldiers, in their rush to push the attack on the remainder of India Company and get more of their troops inside of our lines, left Mike Bednar behind. Alive.

In the chaos, as the Marines dragged as many dead and wounded back up the hill as they could and regrouped on the hilltop, they could see the enemy racing around their left flank to surround them. As thick as the vegetation was, the NVA were close enough to look in the eye. On the right flank the hill dropped off very sharply and was nearly impossible to navigate. India Company was quickly surrounded. There was no escape route. They were seriously outnumbered and in desperate need of ammunition supply and the enemy mortar rounds began to rain down on their very small hilltop.

Only the leaders of that Regiment of the North Vietnamese Army know why they did not finish killing all of India Company. Certainly the U.S. Marines do not. Had the Vietnamese known that by the middle of that first night each Marine was down to his last few rounds of ammunition and had no food, no water, and had they known the extent of the dead and wounded lying on the hill top, I am sure that they would have walked over the top of that hill and killed the remainder of the company. It would not have been difficult.

I am a witness to this story. I was a member of the 1st platoon of I 3/5 and survived those bloody jungle battles.

So, our story begins here, not with the purpose of describing how we got Mike Bednar back, nor of that intense battle and struggle for survival on hill 362 and our near miraculous escape. No, this is not a war story, though I may from time to time describe moments of war. Rather, this story is an attempt to describe our return to that hill 42 years later to find some closure and to place a memorial for the U.S. Marines who died on the hill and at the stream bed two days earlier. The story you are about to read, a combination of Emails to home and journal notes, describes an experience as significant in my life as the war itself, and because of the difficulties and the events that occurred attempting to find and reach that very remote jungle mountain top, perhaps more so. It is the story of a boy who went to war and the man who struggled in his search to find meaning in his life after that war.

Pain is so very hard to write, and some of the worst wounds of war are deeply etched. You cannot see them, hear them or touch them, and the healing of those wounds is a long, lonely battle. A battle that takes a lifetime.

Chapter 2
The Beginning

9:11 pm, June 25, 2007

It's a Monday evening and I'm at home getting ready for bed. An old Marine Corps friend, John Olsen, calls and asks if I would like to return to Vietnam to help place a memorial plaque on Hill 362. This is like a bolt from the sky. It is completely unexpected and I'm momentarily speechless. Hill 362: A name, a place, a scar that has haunted me and chased me my entire adult life. A place I have been running away from for more years than I could count. Finally, I say I will need to discuss it with my wife, Colette. Colette thinks about it for about two minutes, recognizes the opportunity and says "You have to go". I walk around in a daze for the next four weeks as I find out all the particulars.

John has asked 7 other men from India Company to return with him. One is given the task of making/finding a fitting memorial to leave behind. One is asked to document our trip for future review or other causes. I am the only medical Corpsman in the group and I assume the medical role and outline for all what immunizations are needed and what dangers we will face from flora and fauna.

The thought of going back up that hill after all these years is daunting. It is my boogey man. It calls to me from far off in the dark of night. It beckons to me with a sickly finger during times of depression, and each time I respond it stabs me again and again, opening afresh this old and tired scar and I cannot find a way to ignore its call. There are so many ghosts roaming that jungle forest floor. *Lieu chung ta co danh thuc nhung linh hon cua nhung nguoi da*

17

hy sinh? Will we raise the spirits of the dead? Will they welcome us?

John contacted many different people and tour agencies. Our goals are to do a lot of boots on the ground kind of touring, using vehicle transportation as little as possible, as well as to climb up Hill 362 one more time, for a memorial service. The developing plan is to spend a few days in the Chu Lai area looking for places we spent time back in '66, then move farther up the coast to DaNang and west to DongHa and finally into the jungle to climb the hill and spend one or two days on top. Possibly three. We would reverse the order on the way home with two days in SaiGon in lieu of ChuLai for rest and relaxation. We have communicated with ex-pats who live there and many others who have visited recently. We are getting all kinds of conflicting reports on what to expect from the people and the government. Not all of them predict friendliness.

We finally decide on using HaiVenu tour agency. A guide by the name of Ngoc Nguyen has outlined a very detailed trip for us. There are multiple e-mail communications between John and Ngoc which he shares with all of us. She says that there may be some difficulties getting us to our hill 362, but she will do the best she can. The trip may include taking motor scooters from DongHa as far into the jungle as possible and then walking the remainder of the way. She will be teamed with another guide by the name of Thuong, who was somehow involved in the war.

I have emailed all the guys with the CDC recommendations for vaccinations, Malaria prophylaxis and other health related items we need to be concerned about. While we were aware of the incredible heat and humidity, we soon realized that weather conditions would not be our only concerns. The unexploded war ordinances (UXO) still found in the remote areas we are planning to explore, and the many poisonous snakes of the area, particularly Cobras, are constant problems and the cause of many injuries and deaths each year. Nonetheless, it looks like all things are falling in place and we are just waiting for our time to go. To a man, we are anxious and excited, counting the days and E-mailing each other frequently.

Chapter 3

Friday, April 25, 2008

I cannot believe it's time to go already. I have clothes for hiking in hot weather, some camping supplies, including a hammock to suspend between trees for sleeping. I also brought some packaged food and a fair amount of endurance food such as Cliff Bars and Power Bars. I borrowed a great back pack from my nephew and bought some Dominican cigars for the guys. I remember back in '66 I would always carry a box of rum soaked Crooks. The little tiny packs of cigarettes that came in our C-rations were about 20 years old and usually they were moldy. The Crooks were light and easy to pack, and at 19 years old, I loved the sweet taste. Our biggest problem back then was keeping our matches dry. That being the biggest reason that Zippo lighters were so popular.

I have packed and repacked so many times I don't know what I should be taking any more. I am more nervous about this than I was willing to admit. I have no idea what to expect neither from my Marine Corps brothers who I have not seen in all these years, nor from the Vietnamese when we arrive and start tromping through their territory. My schedule is: Friday: Detroit to LA, where most of us will meet up. Saturday: LA to Hong Kong, switch planes, and then on to SaiGon, arriving Sunday night. Monday: early flight from SaiGon to ChuLai where we are slated to spend a few days. From there we will go up the coast to DaNang and then into the jungle by ground. John has collected all monies and booked all flights and guide expenses. He has done just a ton of leg work for this trip. Our guide, Ngoc, has been in near constant contact with John and has reworked our itinerary many times to accommodate us.

Chapter 4
Welcome Back

Friday night. I arrive in LA and head straight across the street from the airport to my hotel. As I enter the hotel, I meet up with Gary Crowell and Stan Guillaume and the three of us grab some beers and head out to the hotel patio. Two great guys and it is very good to see them again.

By Saturday morning most everyone has arrived and we board a huge United Airlines Airbus and take off north over the Cascade Range and a northern route toward Hong Kong. I watch about 5 movies and in between each I am up and walking around trying to meet as many people as I can looking at what appears to be the Bering Sea or Straits and much snow and ice covered water. It is hard to sleep or sit still, I am still quite anxious about this whole trip.

Finally we land at Hong Kong, nearly 15 hours after leaving L.A. We debark and wait around at the airport for another of our group and the next leg onto SaiGon. John tells us that he has invited two more members from India Company on our trip.

A word here about SaiGon, which is now called HoChiMinh City. The older Vietnamese still refer to the city as SaiGon, while the younger generation calls it HoChiMinh City. The vast majority of the Vietnamese population, perhaps over 70% now, was born after the war, which they call The American War. So, most people have no memory of those confusing and violent years. I will probably use both HCMC and SaiGon in my references during this writing.

On board again in Hong Kong, we are on our final leg to SaiGon. We meet the eighth member of our team. The last two will meet us in SaiGon. As we board another United Airlines plane, a Vietnamese flight attendant says to me, "Welcome back!" His name is Omar and he is the first of so many to be gracious and welcoming. Another Vietnamese attendant aboard this flight finds out who we are and is giving us many names and places we should visit. He is a wealth of information about Vietnam, the war, US Army and Marine Corps involvement and many different American and NVA camps. He is excited we are here and he gives me his business card with his email address. His name is Augustus. We call him Auggie.

Word has spread. Before the plane takes off the flight crew announces over the PA who we are, what we're doing here and welcomes us aboard.

It is a relatively short flight to Saigon, about an hour and a half. On the notoriously rough tarmac at Tan Son Nhat Airport in Saigon, we have the smoothest landing I have ever experienced. Not even a ripple. After we land the flight attendants want pictures with us before we leave the plane. It makes me feel like we are on a special mission.

When we leave the airport and hit the street, looking for our guide and the bus to our hotel, we are struck with the intensity of the heat and humidity. It is all consuming. It immediately slows you and weighs on you like a hot, wet blanket. It's one of those things about Vietnam I had forgotten.

Our guide drives us through very congested downtown traffic to The Grand Hotel, situated right on the SaiGon River. It is a majestic place with a pair of gigantic elephant tusks in front of the registration desk and a rooftop bar and restaurant overlooking the river. A great spot. Once we drop our luggage off in our rooms and wash up, we go downstairs to the lobby to meet up and go out for a drink somewhere. The United Airlines flight crew: pilot, copilot and flight attendants, are all standing in the lobby waiting for us!! They want to take us to the top of The Hotel Rex, maybe the most famous social spot in SaiGon, and buy us a drink. I can't believe I went there!!

On our way to the Rex Hotel, we walk past the old SaiGon Opera House, now the HoChiMinh City Municipal Theatre. At one time this building held the Vietnamese House of Parliament after the ouster of the French. It is on the west side of Lam Son Square where the famous picture was taken of the SaiGon Chief of Police executing a Viet Cong officer with his pistol.

The opera house is a magnificent gothic-style French structure, painted brilliant red along its borders and on the upper level façade, and stands in sharp contrast to the new steel and glass high rises that are going up everywhere in the city.

At the large rooftop bar at the top of the hotel, we find out that our United Airlines pilot flew C-140 transport planes here many years ago and the co-pilot is a retired Navy jet fighter pilot. They are quite the pair and true to their calling. The ex-Navy fighter jock is young, animated, excited and full of energy. He is all over the place. The C-140 pilot is calm, slow and deliberate, a very easy going guy. No wonder we had such a perfect landing. He has landed really big planes on the tarmac here hundreds of times.

Mike Carey and Tom Gainer show and so we are now all together:
Mike Carey, Gary Crowell, Gary Campbell, John Olsen, Joe Holt (forever known to us as Private Holt), Manuel

Caro, Tom Gainer, Stan Guillaume, Don Eberle and me. Our ranks have swelled to 10. Gary Campbell is known as "Sarge", Gary Crowell and Mike Carey will be called alternatively by past and present ranks, Lieutenant or Captain/Major, throughout the story. I am called "Doc" by one and all.

We have a great night explaining our stories to the flight crew and we are all very excited and full of energy. Reminiscing begins in earnest and I am so happy to be one of this very special group. Stan, Mike, Tom and I close the night at about 3 am and walk back to The Grand Hotel. We must be up in 3 hours to take our next flight.

Be well,
doug

Chapter 5
Of Purpose and Progress

Our flight to Chu Lai is in a Vietnam Airlines dual prop job and we fly low enough to get good views of the northern delta area around Saigon. The Mekong River flows southeast into Vietnam out of Laos, west of the Annamese Cordillera and spreads out into nine different branches as it approaches Saigon, the delta and the Pacific Ocean. The Annamese range has gently descending slopes on the east side and sharp, precipitous slopes off the western ridges, contributing greatly to the flow of the Mekong. The Vietnamese call these river branches "The Nine Tongues of the Dragon." The shelf that the whole of Southeast Asia sits on tilts ever so slightly off the underlying mantel toward the South China Sea and allows for this very fertile delta and rich abundance of sea foods and rice paddies. It is geographically unique. Through the plane's windows, I try to get as many pictures as I can of the many branches and brackish rivers and the relatively shallow waters that ease out into the ocean. I have never been this far south in Vietnam. I know only the sands of the mid coastal region and the jungle. It is still so hard to believe that today I am headed for a reunion with those areas.

We land at ChuLai without problems and we are the only aircraft on the tarmac. One of the reasons we wanted to land here is that we guarded this air strip as one of our duties for a while back in '66 after Operation Hastings. There is much about ChuLai that seems like home. Once again as the plane circles around to approach the landing strip we are all gawking out the windows, this time searching our memory cells for flashes of days gone by. Lots of sand here.

It is Monday morning, April 29th, and I have been flying off and on for approximately 23 hours since Friday afternoon with another 6 or 7 hours of waiting in airports. Our butts are weary. Here is where we first meet Ngoc and Thuong, our guides. They are waiting outside of the terminal at ChuLai holding a very large, red banner that reads "Welcome Back". They cannot hold this sign up too long for fear of possible government backlash. We are all excited to meet. Ngoc is talkative and has a great smile and is eager to tell us all her plans. She has worked at HaiVenu for 8 years now and this is the most hands-on, boots on the ground type of request she has ever had from American vets or any one. She is very excited to meet us and can't wait to get us started on our journey. Thuong seems somewhat aloof. He does not smile as easily.

One of our guys asks Thuong if he was Viet Cong. We all jump on him pretty quickly. We had been told that asking if someone was Viet Cong can be considered very insulting. We learn very soon that Thuong has quite an extensive history fighting in the Vietnam War and that he most certainly was not Viet Cong.

It's a short ride to our hotel, which is a pretty nice place. The new, modern design looks very out of place directly across the street from the more traditional tin roofed shanties that are typical of the country. Of course the beds are box springs only, no mattresses and only a box spring cover without sheets but I don't think I'm going to mind so much. It's off the floor and it looks clean. I'm in Chu Lai, Vietnam. How much can I ask for, anyway? Someone quickly arranges for us all to get blankets and a pillow. I wonder what the heck I'm going to do with a blanket in 100 degree heat and 75 to 80 percent humidity.

During the afternoon we sit across the street near the beach under a thatched roof, open air cafe with a concrete slab floor and drink Vietnamese beer. They don't have cold beer but eventually start putting some on ice for us. I'm thinking that I will eat/drink anything they give me. I will try not to care about heat/humidity or how tired I am or how far we walk. I will try to accept this country and its people as is. I am here in friendship and deep humility and I am here for a single purpose.

We are having a riot with each other, renewing bonds, telling and retelling the same old lies about each other and, of course, reliving all our memories of so many military operations and fire fights and especially of those several days on Operation Hastings. Each of us tries to describe as graphically as possible our experiences. We want to remember every detail and to get every one's singular story. What we did. What we saw. Where we were. It is our purpose for being here. We want to know/remember where each of our guys died and how. This is not morbid on our part. We are not trying to regale ourselves with blood and gore stories. Of course we do, but this is therapeutic. These things happened to us. Physical trauma aside, the mental trauma takes years to process. When you are literally face to face with your enemy, close enough to curse and yell at this enemy through the thick, triple canopy jungle, the memory is indelibly imprinted on every part of your being. The human mind can accept only so much terror at one time.

On that fateful day of July 24th 1966, there was a thick blanket of low lying, heavy rain clouds with off and on periods of rain from Typhoon Ora. It was difficult to hear anything with the rain dripping through the jungle trees, and that night our visibility, literally, was less than 12 inches. The ambush began about 11am. By 8 pm it was as dark a night as I had ever witnessed.

Some time that night Lt. Crowell coaxed a spotter plane, a small Piper Cub, to circle our area and drop flares about every 20-30 minutes. Occasional bits of light in the inky darkness to give us something to focus on and to give us a ray of hope. As the flares swung down, falling to earth beneath their small parachutes, the light reflected off the jungle trees and downed timber, making for a most eerie effect, with shadows swaying to and fro as if everything was moving. As I think back on that now, our fire discipline was incredibly strong, a testament to our training, our trust in each other and to the incredibly brave leadership of our platoon commanders who seemed to be everywhere. Our situation was pretty bleak. We were fighting mostly with hand grenades, using what little M-14 ammunition we had as sparingly as possible. We were completely surrounded, with no escape route. We did not have enough healthy Marines to form an adequate perimeter, so the platoon commanders put at least one wounded Marine in each fighting hole, some fighting holes had two wounded together and some of those fighting holes were nothing more than K-bar scratchings in the stony dirt. We had piled what dead Marines we could drag up the trail near the top with most of the seriously wounded next to them and tried to dig protective holes for them as well. I remember worrying about how exposed they were and how in God's name we were going to get down that trail to search for anyone else. At the time, in all of the chaos, I did not realize Frank was missing.

 It was clear what everyone was thinking, and as we awaited the next volley of attacks from the enemy, Gunnery Sergeant Glenn came around to each position and told us to destroy all of our personal effects and all identification except for our Geneva Convention cards which identified us as property of the United States Government. As Gunny left my hole that night I did not, at first, understand the implications of what he had just instructed us to do. It was not until later, while trying to find a wounded Marine in that absolute pitch black darkness and having a grenade thrown at me, that I realized that none of us would be seeing our homes and families again and that we would not be returning to the U.S.S. Pickaway and the other ships that brought us across the Pacific Ocean. We were surrounded and outnumbered and there was no reason to think that the enemy would simply give up or go away. In an odd sense of naïveté, I wondered how the Navy was going to return to the U.S. with empty ships. Surely our ghosts would be staying on this wretched hill. It was apparent to all of us that it was just a matter of time before the enemy would come sweeping over the top to devour the remainder of us. While they fought us, probed us and harassed us all night long however, the NVA did not mount an attack strong enough to break through our lines. To those of us who survived, it still makes no sense.

Very early the next morning, July 25th, we had had no contact with the enemy for a couple of hours and began hearing a voice down the trail yelling: "Marines. Help me. Marines." At first we thought it was a ploy by the NVA to lure some of us out; however a quick decision was made to send a patrol forward on the chance it was one of our men. What we discovered was Mike Bednar, alone, crawling up the side of the trail holding his intestines in with his hands. Once Mike was back inside our lines another patrol was formed to search for and recover any other Marines left outside of the perimeter and to recon the NVA positions. That patrol went forward, into the area where the ambush began. As that patrol was returning, the remainder of the force of the North Vietnamese Army had regrouped and was taking a southwestern approach towards our rear on its way back up the hill to attack us again and complete its task. Lima Company, also of our 3rd Battalion, 5th Marines, was just arriving on the scene, approaching from the southeast side, to lend support and those men walked smack dab into the NVA just as they were approaching our lines, surprising both sides as well as us, and another intense fire fight ensued causing the NVA to finally retreat. It was during this final skirmish that the NVA used some sort of chemical or poison gas to advance their position. Fortunately, whatever that gas was had minimal destructive effect. Had Lima Company not been there, we would never have been able to hold them off and would not be here today and this revisit would not be taking place. It takes a while to process it all and being able to talk about the worst parts is cathartic. We just can't do this stuff back home with civilians. The reason we are here is to honor our friends and fighting mates who gave their lives. To my knowledge, India Company's list of commendations for just those 96 hours in 1966 include: 118 Purple Hearts, 4 Bronze Stars, 3 Silver Stars, 1 Navy Cross and 1 Congressional Medal of Honor. We are a much decorated group and we are forever indebted to Lima Company. In retrospect, there are not enough medals to reward the multiple acts of selfless bravery that occurred on that hill top. Many of those acts were never recorded or reported.

Be well,
doug

Chapter 6
Children

About 2 pm we bus out to a remote area to find hill 66, the villages of Long Phu 1 and Long Phu 2, as well as some other areas we patrolled after Operation Hastings. We get off the bus and trek through back roads and trails. An old man comes out of his house and hands Gary Campbell an American dog tag. We pass an elementary school and the children inside are practicing an alphabet or numbers or something, in unison. Soon, they become aware that we are outside and they all come out to see us. Laughing and nearly all waving the peace sign at us, shouting in English "Hello! How are you?" Everyone here now is taught English as a second language. Years ago it was Russian. Before that, French. We take many pictures of the children and to a man we are impressed with their bright faces and energy. What amazing smiles these children have. The fact that the school compound is ringed with barbed wire is puzzling to us. Later on we decide that we will make a monetary gift to the school. Perhaps tomorrow or the next day. We spent considerable time in this area around the end of 1966. We provided health care on an almost daily basis and helped guard that year's rice harvest for the local farmers, so we feel a very special connection to the Long Phu villages.

Walking through small villes and hamlets gives us a haunting sense of remembrance. Flashes of time gone by. Not all of it is bad, but the memories surface with a heightened sense of awareness that comes from having been in a life and death struggle - a lesson that never leaves. We remember hedge lines of cacti, palm and betel nut trees, and we remember walking along the elevated paths between rice paddies, feeling over exposed and vulnerable.

As we walk from hamlet to hamlet, the word gets passed around about a group of Americans, and many of the villagers try to sneak peeks at us. The children collect in groups of 5 or 6 and giggle at us. This is a shy culture and they have little expectation other than daily needs. There are few demands on them. Their civility is so deep, so basic. It could not exist in the western world. I can't help but wonder how they can be so calm, so open, and so polite after 100 years of war.

We'll spend another day or two here on the outskirts of Chu Lai looking for some old haunts and that will be the last of life on the coast for us as we head in toward the jungle and our goal.

Be well,
Doug

Chapter 7
Hammocks on the Beach

Back at the hotel and again we all head over to the rickety cafe across the street for more beer. Gary Campbell breaks not one but two of the tiny little plastic chairs because he can't learn to not lean back in them. I have pictures!! We are all laughing so hard it hurts. We are beginning to relax and sense just how therapeutic this visit may be.

Joe Holt is just an amazing guy. He's an incredible story teller, a remarkable finder of lost souls and pretty much a straight shooter. He has a gift. He has us in stitches every time he says something and by now all he has to do is open is mouth and we all start smiling. We know it's gonna be funny.

Late that night I find myself alone with Mike Carey. He smokes a black and tan cigar that reminds me of my old rum soaked Crooks. I have a smoke with him and as the evening wears on I ask him questions about religion, faith and carousing/cussing. He is one of the saltiest, toughest Marines I have ever met. He won two Silver Star commendations, back to back on Operation Hastings alone and has another Silver Star for a later engagement. After three tours in Vietnam and retiring from the Marine Corps, both he and my platoon leader, Sam Williams became Episcopal priests. We talk for hours about Christ, the scriptures and the Christian church. We discuss other religions and western vs. eastern cultures. Mike lives in Guam and says he cannot stand the constant rush and anxiety that permeates our society. My respect for this man is boundless and certainly has not been diminished on this night. We are such a lucky group to have him.

Mike and I arrange with the cafe owner to use their hammocks and stay right there on the beach. We each give her 300,000 Dong, which is about $40 US. She probably has not seen this much money at one time in quite a while, if ever, and certainly not two Americans wanting to sleep at her simple cafe. We talk ourselves to sleep gently swaying in Vietnamese hammocks overlooking the western shore of the Pacific Ocean. Sunrise over the Pacific the next morning is a sight to behold. At this point I feel a tether let go, and I say to myself that it would be easy to stay here.

Some of us begin to talk about buying a piece of land and building a hotel on the north side of ChuLai in a little cove we spotted. We realize that in 20 years the cafes will all be gone and it will be all tourist centers and resorts. We know it is farfetched, but why not? Why not us?

Chapter 8
Contact

The next day we have pho (rice noodle soup) for breakfast and we are off in search of another area we traveled long ago.

Lots of walking today in deeper and deeper countryside and rice paddies. I am now getting many flashes of past images and I'm amazed that I am here. Already my western world seems a distant memory. This is a remarkable bookend to my last adventure in this land.

Everyone finds us curious. Everyone is friendly and helpful. Late in the afternoon we are trying to find a way to get across a small river that we thought would be dried up at this time of the year. An older man in camos appears out of nowhere and tells us exactly how and where to cross. He has a look in his eyes that very clearly tells me he has seen many of us before long ago on a very different mission. He is friendly but aloof until he gives Stan a big high five when Stan asks to take his picture.

We are very unsure that we've found some of the old outposts we are looking for, hill 22 or Red Hill, and the sun is starting to get lower in the sky. On our way back to the main road, another man who followed us for about 1/2 hour from afar approaches us and informs our guide that he was Viet Cong and that he worked this area from 1960 to 1975. We have struck gold!! We all talk, hold hands and hug until dark and then decide to see if we can find him again tomorrow because he tells us we are not on Red Hill. It occurs to us that he could probably tell us exactly where each of our bunkers were those 40-odd years ago.

Back at the hotel/resort Ngoc and Thuong have found a place for us to eat at one of the little cafes across the street, and we are not disappointed. We are promised prawns, squid, tuna and local vegetables. Everything BBQ'd. Everything just brought in from the sea. The prawn is served first and we're told there are 2 apiece. I pull the first prawn off the plate and it is every bit of 7 inches long. Had to weigh a full pound! The calamari is the best I have ever had. Huge, tasty and delicate. I am eating skin and everything of the tuna. Good to a degree I cannot explain. This meal cost us $11 US!! The owner, a woman, walks over to Mike Carey, points at the tattoo on his forearm and says "USMC. I work for them many years ago."
Tonight I have no taste for drink or smoke. I am beat and I need sleep. There will be more.

Be well,
Doug

Chapter 9
Liberation and Anticipation

April 30, 2008

It is the end of April and it is Vietnam Liberation Day. This is a huge holiday here with May Day to follow. Kids are out of school. There is a sense of holiday in the air. Someone has set Vietnam flags all the way up and down the road through the city. Bright red, with the yellow star; very colorful. I am staying at the cafe for the morning to catch up on my diary and wash clothes. I'll go out again with the group in the afternoon. We have decided to eat at the same cafe tonight. Crabs are on the menu!!!

Some free thought:
Images of life in this small village: Gaggle of geese walking into and out of the café and on down the street. Every dog looks like it is from the same litter. The dogs are not petted nor do they follow any specific single person. Fishing boats out all night, all day. Children playing in the sand, practicing break dancing skills. Everyone on scooters, bicycles or walking. Nearly everyone with something to sell. I see natural passion in the young adults. Natural energies. But the inner calmness is at once disarming and alluring. The geese are back again, loudly proclaiming their right to cross the road and re-enter the cafe. Nearly every woman on the road or in the fields here wears hat, kerchief over face and long sleeves and gloves. Perhaps 25% of the men wear masks. I find out later that the reason is to protect skin color. Like many places in the world, lighter skin is valued because it means that one is wealthy enough to avoid working in the fields.

It is amazing how much a person can carry on a little scooter. I mean really amazing. Whole families: babies, children, and adults, everyone on one motorbike. Multiple huge boxes piled way high over their heads, 30-40 live ducks all tied by the feet. You never know what you'll see. Just amazing.

A clean, neat new military vehicle just went by with two men in uniform and I see it turning around. I know I am out of place here and I wonder if they heard an American is sitting alone in a cafe. We are still not sure how the officials will accept us during this trip.

If I sit here long enough, some will ride or walk by just to see what I look like. They all slow down as they pass.

The women and children are striking in their appearance. Beautiful, soft, light brown skin, large brown eyes staring straight at you with that inner calmness that they all have, totally unguarded, and as if they can see right through you.

The longer I sit here, the more young children stop to ask if I will buy one of their coconuts. I know they do not expect me to buy. They want to get as close as they can to see my features, maybe talk and touch me. They write their names and ages in my journal and we try to speak to each other in what few words we know of each other's language.

The military vehicle, a jeep type, has now passed by 3 times. I look, but the driver will not reciprocate. Perhaps I am not on his radar.

ChuLai is a crossroads of city and country on the central coast, south of DaNang. I see nothing here taller than two stories with one exception. The local bank has a tower, three stories. Money is the same everywhere. Modernity will find its way here, not because the people are looking, pressing for it but because its inexorable creep will find them. I am not altogether happy with that thought.

To the outsider, so much of the culture and people here appear the same, but they are not. This is a widely diverse grouping of ancient cultures and tribes significantly influenced by Thailand and China.

Every minute here the pace of life is settling inside of me, together with the realization of how far south I am and how different this culture is. I am finding some real peace. The tethers continue to let go.

Tomorrow we head out for a stopover in DaNang, then on to DongHa and west, into the weeds. To a man, we are sorry to leave ChuLai. It feels so much a part of us. Again, like home. This will be the heart of the trip now. There are lots of questions about logistics and where we will spend the nights. John and Stan both have GPS systems which are giving them trouble. John is now saying we will go up our hill and back down on the same day and perhaps again the next. The original plan was to go up and spend between one and three days on top. Ngoc is trying to make sure there will be no political problems. The plan keeps changing due to logistics and politics. And we are getting many warnings from everyone in the area that there are many poisonous snakes in that region, particularly cobras, as well as a ton of unexploded ordinance. I am of a mind to get right up hill 362 as quickly as possible and just stay there until they tell me I have to leave. My only goals are to face that hill top and to let my brothers know that we have not forgotten them. I know I am not alone in those thoughts.

If I listen to the ghosts on that hill howl at night
will it give me strength
or sap me of my purpose?

These self-same ghosts,
the riders of my dreams
creeping ever closer now.

For whom do they howl?
Is it for themselves?
Or is it for me?

Mike says he'll stay up there with me if I'd like. Actually, that would be the best scenario for me. Mike is probably the only one here that I could open that last door with. Will I have the strength to free that damn beast that has ridden my heart all these years? Already every hair on my body is standing erect and we can't even see the mountain yet.

Chapter 10
DaNang

Wow! DaNang has changed. What a huge city this is: Masses of people, traffic jams, huge hotels and banks, and construction is everywhere. It gives every impression of a modern city hustle and bustle. I had only been here one time during my tour of duty and that was when one of my brothers had been in a bad car accident. He was apparently close enough to death that my family requested that I come home. The U.S. government, in its great wisdom, had me taken out of the fighting and planted me at the DaNang Air Base where I was to await my brother's fate. If he died, I got to go home. If he did not, I would be returned to my unit. The ensuing 48 hours was an existential nightmare. Thankfully, he did not die.

DaNang is built on the beach of a long, narrow inlet, the southern part of which is called China Beach. There was a popular TV show about it and the war. The sand is so light, soft and very fine, made of white coral. No huge waves or undercurrents. What a perfect place for resorts/hotels.

Our destination is the Furama Resort. We're told it is the only 5 star hotel we will get on this trip, and it meets the criteria. Built just north of China Beach, with new resorts being built both north and south, it is a gorgeous place. Our passports are taken as we enter; we are offered drinks and asked to sit while our stay is arranged. Soon, we are escorted to our rooms where our luggage is already delivered and there are more free drinks, all sorts of fresh fruits and other foods for our enjoyment. Huge bath room with separate shower and Jacuzzi, tub, large sink, toilet. There are arrays of robes we can wear and sandal type footwear that are ours to keep. Between the main building and the beach there is a large wading/swimming pool that looks like it's lined with the deepest green jade I have ever seen. The shoreline is another 40-50 yards. The Pacific is cool, not cold, and very calm. The grounds are just covered with all sorts of flowery and colorful plants. There are little alcoves and gardens around every corner, some that you can't figure out how to get to and all constantly being attended to by a myriad of people. Every plant has a different type and color of flower.

We head straight to the bar and order up some drinks which turn out to be pretty pricey. Beers are $4-5 dollars American. Already we are spoiled. Someone tells us that the hotel cost is about $110 per night, American. Hard to believe. This is the kind of place where you expect to see movie stars and other rich and famous people.

By now we are running out of cigars and the ones here at the Furama are incredibly expensive. They are all Cuban and I'm sure all good, but they are expensive. They know they have a lock on this commodity. If you walk the streets of the city asking where to buy cigars, everyone shows you cigarettes or Phillies Panatelas. Apparently, there is little else. Well, we will head out west and into the bush tomorrow and we'll just have to get used to no cigars.

Here is our first access to computers and much of my time is spent corresponding, crafting these letters home, trying to convey images of our trip and this lush country. The remainder of time is spent in the bar where the bar maids are all young and attractive in their *ao dai's*. I befriend a young bar maid named Hien who calls me "my doctor." She lives with her parents, works days at the resort and attends school in the evenings, studying international hotel management and tourism. She is generous and kind and she has offered to take me around town on her scooter after work. While this offer is tempting, I know that the resort forbids employees to fraternize with guests after hours and I politely turn her down. I know this is an innocent offer on her part and that she could probably show me things about DaNang that I could get nowhere else, but I feel I must do what is right and safe for her position.

Later that afternoon we head out walking to a cafe John discovered in his attempts to get contacts here. Called Tam's Pub, it is run by a woman named Tam Ky (pronounced Tom Kee) who is trying to break into the tourist/guide industry. As we walk through town, a group of 5 or 6 women begin following us, some walking, some on scooters, all asking our names and if they can take us to their father's shops to buy marble or other wares. Of course we're thinking they are looking for something else. When we arrive at Tam's Pub, it is something of a surf and burger shop ala America and the women that followed us walk right in and sit down in chairs near our table. They sit and talk to each other watching our every move. It is clear that they will follow us out and back to the resort when we leave. They are persistent but while we are at the café they are polite. They do not hound us with questions or requests. They just sit and watch us.

We meet Tam and she is just wonderful; big smiles and pretty good English. Enough so that we can all converse. She tells us a bit about her life and her shop. She is very happy to have us here. Most of the guys order the American style food on her menu, burgers and stuff. I stick with the local cuisine and am rewarded with a great dinner of assorted seafood with calamari, of course, and local veggies.

While eating and having some beers at Tam's, a young couple in bathing suits come in with their surf boards, looking American and speaking English, all sandy and wet, as though just off the surf and they go into the back of the café toward the kitchen. A tall American couple comes in and they are introduced to us. Apparently good friends of Tam, the woman, a physical therapist, and her husband sold everything they had and moved here from America to do some work training physical therapists in the DaNang area. Her name is Virginia Lockett and she is a wealth of information about the place. Her husband, Dave, is a photographer. Remarkably, she tells us that the women who are following us really do want to take us to their parent's shops and sell us some of their marble, nothing more. She says there is virtually no crime in DaNang and these women will take any one anywhere any time of night or day. And indeed, when we leave that night they follow us back to the resort needling us with questions about our lives and requests to accompany them to their shops.

We are all tired when we get back. We have a couple of drinks at the bar and off to bed. Tomorrow some of us will take a 5 hour train ride west toward the Lao border, the rest of us will go by bus which is a bit shorter ride. I have decided to take the train, along with Mike, Gary Crowell, Pvt Holt, John and Thuong. One of my main goals on this trip is to immerse myself in the Vietnamese culture and with these people. I want to see what they see, eat what they eat, walk where they walk. Before I retire, I head back to the bar and secretly buy a half dozen cigars. I will surprise Stan and Gary deep in the jungle when they start to dream of getting back to the cities and access to cigars, cold beers and good scotch with ice cubes.

Be well,
Doug

Chapter 11
Of Trains and Sorrows

May 2, 2008

We are much farther inland now. Vietnam is only about 50 Kilometers wide here along the old DMZ. Looking out the window of the train as we leave the coastal area and head inland toward the gentle eastern slopes of the Annamese range and the jungle, I get to watch the slow change of vegetation and elevation and I find myself alone with my thoughts as I watch the landscape go by. It is an interesting mix of sand, swamp and lush vegetation, rising to low mountain jungles. This is such a beautiful country. It looks so rich and deep and yet my memories are nightmares.

Back in 1968 I was unable to provide myself with any real perspective on my psychological condition when returning home and I became a very lost soul. I tried to go to school but found I could not concentrate on my studies. I began to dabble in drugs and I wandered all across the country, hitch-hiking from East coast to West and back several times, taking multiple menial jobs and panhandling in the cities in between. As the years went by the dreams and self-loathing and guilt of surviving still did not abate and my drug use and living on the periphery of society worsened. I was lost. I kept my guilt and shame buried deeply so that no one would know. No one would suspect, and it would never have to be talked about. I had no goals, no aims. Living day to day not knowing or really caring what the next day brought. It was a period of my life that I did so many things that I now regret. I was still able to see the difference between good people and bad but I no longer cared. So many people wanted to ask questions I was not ready or was unable to answer. So many of the questions insulting or naive. It was easy to be resentful. Hating myself made it easy to hate society and hate the government that sent me into that war. It made it easier to commit those regrettable acts and to put the needles in my arms. Only in retrospect can I say that what I was trying to do was to stop the memories, to bury the guilt of surviving, to blur the image I saw every day in the mirror telling me I was not brave enough and to keep those dreams and visions of mortars and death and dismembered bodies at bay in my fitful sleep.

Silence has been my enemy since I left the war. The deafening silence that occurs in the dead of night or when I am all alone. That same silence that allows the monster that sits on my heart to come alive and expose itself and again reopen that old and tired scar. It has been a heavy load to bear and I am so very lucky that after many years of living on the streets, I was unsuccessful in my attempt at medicinal suicide and somehow eventually began to get a more rational sense of self and begin a somewhat normal course of living that allowed me to get through schooling and provide myself with some stability.

Today, as we make our way westward over the *HiVu* Pass and the many old, decaying French military bunkers that lay along this ridge, my mind wanders and I think of how long ago it was, that other life of mine. How young and innocent we were. And I begin to feel a sense of tragedy and perhaps some self-pity. Who knows what our lives would have been like had we not gone up that hill? Or what my life would have been like without all those years of attempted slow suicide. Drugs, alcohol, cigarettes and lying were the addictions I used to help cover up my shame, to hide my guilt. I would gladly trade death on the hill to escape the spurs of the demon that drives my dreams. These are the leftover dredges of the wretched rend of my war. All of the things not done or not said, all of the remorse. It is like walking blindfold through a quicksand field of emotion.

Yes, Vietnam tore out a piece of my soul and I have never been able to staunch the bleeding. My aim over the next few days is to retrieve that torn piece of soul and try to rid myself of this old and deep wound. I will find a way to patch myself together and I have made myself believe that a patch-work soul is better than none. I feel the stirrings of a true sense of conviction and singular purpose, powerful and subtle as I head west, helping to steel me for the coming days and the anxiety of facing my demons. I peer out of the window and into the eyes of every rice and manioc worker we pass. Do they know that I am here? Do they know what I am after? What I long to steal back from them? Will I be able to recognize that part of myself that I left here so very long ago? I am certain of where to look. Absolutely certain. And we are getting closer to that very spot with every clickety-clack of this slow moving train.

Hill 362

Once upon a time
I shared my head
with a creature so vile
living under my bed and
in my life
Full of smoke
and breathing fire
It did not care what life I led nor let me be
and ruled me with an iron fist instead of living
and allowing my true destiny
Along the way
I lost a sense of self
and did not know where I belonged
and did not know or how to use
The ground beneath my feet and
Right and wrong
But as I grew I began to sew
the patches of a life together
with good times and bad
I said goodbye to wayward boys
and drugs
and suicidal toys
and still could not decide
on what was home and where
just where did I have to roam
to find
where I belonged
Looking for that place I hid
before the monster's storm
that took my soul
and left it there upon that hill
back when I was
just a kid.

Chapter 12
DongHa

Upon arrival at the Dong Ha train station it is not exactly
clear where to go when we get off the train. We are on one
of the middle tracks and there is no walkway to guide us
and we see no buildings, so we follow the locals and after
crossing a few tracks and going around a couple sets of
train cars we see the station building. In the parking lot is
the bus with the remainder of our group, waiting for us.
The DongHa market is right next to the train station and we
take some time to check out the scenery and what the
market has to offer. Both Joe Holt and I are on the hunt for
a knife of some sort to take into the jungle with us. I am a
curious wanderer and am soon lost in this huge
indoor/outdoor market. I buy a bottle of some sort of liquor
that has a cobra snake in it, hood expanded, with the tail of
yet another cobra in its teeth. Wild, weird, whacky. Just
what I need to take home. I have some money set aside for
trinkets for everyone at home but I want to buy on the
down swing of our trip, not before we get into the jungle. I
have only so much room in my backpack. By the time I get
back to the bus everyone is yelling at me for taking so long.
I am getting a reputation for wandering off. I never did
find a knife of decent enough quality to buy.

The Dong Truong Son Hotel is quite a bit nicer than we
expected for the little town of DongHa. The area around
Dong Ha was nearly obliterated back in the war years, as
was most every place in QuangTri Province. Heavy
fighting, heavy bombing, heavy casualties all over this
area. It is also the poorest province in Vietnam. It may
always be so.

There is something of a Karaoke set up at our hotel and
during the evening a group of us wander down and sit in a

small room with a karaoke machine and some of the locals. They take their Karaoke seriously here in Asia. Karate can be interpreted as "without fist," Karaoke as "without orchestra." People take turns singing songs and you can get song lyrics in about a hundred languages. At the end of the song the machine gives you a grade on how well you performed. Gary Crowell and I sing the old Ritchie Valens tune "Donna," and we score a 98. The best score of the night. Any time you buy a beer in this room, everyone gets one, on you. You have to be careful. Much later that evening a couple of very young local girls come in bumping and grinding, wanting to dance. They can't be a minute over 18. It's very clear that they are looking for something else as well. We are finding their gyrations and energy level hilarious, particularly in light of their futility. We can at least buy them a beer.

Tomorrow we are off into the jungle and searching for our hill. There is still no set plan in place. Logistics and politics are trickier than we had expected. We are getting information that there is some sort of political upheaval at the Lao border, very near where we plan to travel. We will have to play it all by ear. Ngoc is willing to try anything we want.

Be well,
Doug

Chapter 13
Drink up

May 3, 2008

You can hear the jungle before you enter. In Southeast Asia the Cicadas and birds and other insects combine to make a high pitched whine not unlike using a circular saw. You almost don't notice it at first and it builds and builds until you are asking yourself where the saw mill is and when you realize it is everywhere, the immensity and completeness of it is staggering. It's almost like a warning sign.

We are now very close to the Lao border and the 17th parallel. It's amazing that it seems like familiar territory. As we leave Hwy 9 and start down a dirt road, we approach The Rockpile and Razor Back Ridge. This is it. The reason we are here is to climb over Razorback one more time and attempt a climb onto that hill we call 362. We have asked them to stop the bus so we can get pictures of these two mountain structures, not thinking that we will be almost on top of them in another day. We are struck by the feeling of Deja vu. We've traveled this valley, these mountains. Flashes of memory come in waves. I don't know about the other guys, but I have goose bumps.

Finally, we leave the bus and start walking. We are walking into the jungle and we're told that once again plans have changed. We are to spend the next two nights near a minority village. These are Lao mountain people who were relocated here in 1975 to have better conditions. After a short trek, we enter the village, basically a large clearing in the dense foliage and we see that all the houses are on stilts and have thatched roofs. There is no electricity, no roads. The men are standing in front of their houses. We see very few women and most of the children are indoors or standing far back and sneaking peeks at us out of the window openings and around corners. We're told they are extremely shy and that we cannot take pictures at this time. When we turn to face them, they run or hide.

This is a patriarchal society. The men do not work. The women wear sarongs and work in the fields growing rice, corn and tapioca/manioc. They catch fish in a nearby river and grow chickens for meat and eggs. There are chickens everywhere around the village. Pigs are too expensive. There is a small school for primary education built 4 years ago where they learn the three R's. Most teenagers get married by 15 or 16 and so do not attend much high school, where English is taught. To attend high school would be a long trek to another village. They speak two languages, their own Lao mountain dialect and Vietnamese.

On our first day, we plant new trees along the main path way and at the school. This is very exciting for them and the children begin to get closer. At first when we turned to face them, they would run away very quickly, but eventually, they stay and stare at us, clinging to each other for comfort. I try to be as respectful as possible, addressing each person straight forward saying "*xin chao*", a respectful hello in Vietnamese. The children yell after me with a traditional greeting for a respected elder, "*chao bac,* " and it gives me a very deep sense of comfort and immediate respect for this mountain culture. Later in the day as our tents were being set up, I walk back into the village with Ngoc and talk with some of the women and children. I took off my hat and sunglasses and many of the children went wide eyed. Some of them had not seen a blue-eyed person before. The women all talked at once to Ngoc, asking how that could be. They are told it is because of my reddish hair color and she urges them to come close and look at the hair on my arms. Later we make a gift to the village of books for the school, a soccer ball, a volleyball and net, and some toys for the children. The young men immediately take to the volleyball and it's obvious they have played this before.

It is unbelievably hot here today, easily 100 degrees, with high humidity and not a cloud in the sky. I am surprised that I had forgotten about this heat. It is debilitating. That evening we are treated to an incredibly special ceremony. The villagers all come out, make a big bonfire out of bamboo near our camp and spread mats on the ground in a long row. Large ceremonial pottery urns are brought out which contain fermented rice wrapped in banana leaves. The village elder sticks many very long (about 3-4 feet) hollow reeds into these orange colored urns and young people begin to pour water into them. Once full, the oldest male beckons us all to drink, saying, *"boc moi, boc moi"* and every one sucks the liquid through the straws. I am amazed at the complex taste of this juice. It's sweet and has a depth very much like sherry or port. As we drink, the young people continue to fill the urns with water. Only the village elders and our group are allowed to drink this potion. The main group of villagers do not. Soon, the villagers start singing. At the end of each song everyone claps and the older men beckon us to drink. *"Boc moi, boc moi."* Gary Crowell urges us to sing as well and our first song is "Row, row, row your boat." What a hoot! Sung in two part harmony, the villagers went wild. They loved it. We began trading songs back and forth and drinking and eating a combination of candy, rice cakes, dried fish and some sort of sausage they make. This is like a National Geographic experience – awesome, unreal, unexpected, inspiring, and more. The glow of the bonfire gives it a magical lighting. It is nearly overwhelming. It's obvious that the villagers are excited about us being there and are showing appreciation. Our interpreter tells us they have not done this for any one in many years.

The children are taking interest in me because I was introduced *as "bac si"* or doctor. Perhaps the blue eyes also had something to do with it. The children are following us everywhere now, and I am getting some great pictures. They ask if anyone would like to spend the night in the village. I immediately agree. I want to completely immerse myself in this culture. They have prepared a house for me and after the ceremony I grab my hammock and head to the house. The custom is that the home owners clean the house out and find another place to sleep to allow the guest privacy. So I sleep in this house in the middle of the village, alone, my sweat drip, drip, dripping from the low point of my hammock onto the wooden floor. Of course when I get up to leave in the morning, about 5am, everyone is watching me.

Chapter 14
Tigers and Snakes and Stars, oh my!

I forgot about the sky at night here. The sky is ablaze with brilliance. I am far enough south that I can see the North Star and the Southern Cross in the same sky along with big and little dippers, Orion, Scorpio. I wish I could recognize more. You can see shooting stars every few minutes. The planets look like full moons back home on a saturday night and you become acutely aware of how massive the universe is and how very small we are. Study the stars, my friends.

The villagers had 4 of the young adults stay out near our camp for us. They said there were occasionally wild animals and wanted to protect us. The guys told me that these young men got up about every hour and walked around the tents. They also had some herbs that we spread around our tents as repellants for the snakes.
During the war years, the elephant and tiger population receded into Laos and Cambodia. Over the past few years they are beginning to expand their territories and are coming back into Vietnam. The villagers have reported seeing tigers they estimated at 3 meters in length.

We've been eating MRE's and dehydrated camping food for 2 days and getting pretty used to it again. Not bad stuff, especially if you have a little hot sauce to pump it up. We all still dream of having those massive prawns back in Chu Lai. We know we will stop in Hue on the way back; perhaps there will be good food there as well. I keep expecting to come across something that doesn't agree with me, but so far, the food has been outstanding.

love to all,
doug

Chapter 15
Nervous Relief

I do not know what day it is, it might be Saturday, but this day we make our attempt on the hill which means we will go over Razor Back ridge and head into that mountainous territory for the 2nd time in 42 years. We are excited and nervous. We make sure we have our memorial stuff and we head out just like Marines, in formation. We had a frightening scare on this trip and I will write about it and more next time. We are all safe, not all well, but we will all make it back with memories of a lifetime. As strange as it may seem, I was not really all that worried about dangers prior to this trip and now I am so very thankful that we are all still alive and on our way back.

As of now we are off to DongHa, (I need to find some medicine for one of our guys,) then back to the luxury resort in DaNang the next day and then on to SaiGon. That is supposed to be the "vacation" part of the trip but after a very emotional day attempting to get up 362, it may take us some time to want to celebrate. My camera stopped functioning on the attempt to make the hill, but I have many, many pictures so far. Can't wait to share them with you all.

Love to all,
Doug

Chapter 16
The Hill

**9 Good Men
In front of Razorback Ridge**

Well, here it is, and it's not pretty.
May 4th, 6:00 AM.

Once back at the bus we head out onto a two track road and go as far as the vehicle will allow. It's now time to saddle up and get on with it. We are all very excited about getting to the hill and planting our shrines. Joe Holt has a marble plaque that he wanted to bury and of course we have the stones with the names of those who died on the hill. We also have stones for those who lost their lives in the stream bed the two nights before and are hoping we can reach both spots, but 362 is our main goal. Each stone is slightly smaller than baseball size. The excitement is palpable.

Joe tells us early in the morning that he has decided not to attempt the climb. He doesn't want to slow us down and he really doesn't think he can make it. I know this was a difficult decision for him. He will stay back with the bus and wait for us. I immediately approach Manuel, hoping that news will give him second thoughts as well. Since learning about his health issues, I fear for his well-being. However, he is adamant about going and confident that he can make it.

About 6:30 am we begin the climb around the Rockpile and over Razor Back. I am in the middle, 5th, as always. Manuel is in front of Don Eberle who is in front of me. This is good; I can keep a close eye on Manny. Everyone is chipper and excited. We have a local tribal guide with us who says he knows where we are going. We're still very unsure about our coordinates. We are warned several times by Ngoc and the local guide about the unexploded ordinance and snakes and not to wander off and to stay in single file on any trail we might find. Explosives of every description, hand grenades, booby traps, land mines, cannon shells and aircraft bombs from 250 to 1000 pounds are said to be everywhere, the most common being cluster bombs. Snakes and ERW/UXO (Explosive Remnants of War/Unexploded Ordinance), are major concerns. Regardless, I am excited and happy. This is really all I came here for. All any of us came here for. This day. This hill. I worked hard in my preparation. I did my morning training runs at home with a pack on my back, all the while envisioning stepping over that ridge top. I didn't want to leave anything to chance. While knowing that I have a lot of unanswered questions and anxieties about finding myself on top of 362, still, I am feeling a positive excitement. I am right now very willing to face those questions and anxieties. Today I feel strong enough to do this.

On the very first hill I see Manuel take his hat off and use his hands to push on his knees as we climb. We've only just begun. Stan, Don and Sarge are all already sweating buckets. Don and Sarge are both dressed in heavy cotton. Manny's clothes look heavy, too, and he has on heavy leather boots. This hiking wear, while similar to government-issue 42 years ago, is not practical today. I realize that I did not adequately prepare them about this aspect and the need for a lengthy exercise regimen to prepare for this trip and bringing high-tech, breathable light-weight clothes.

By the third hill I start asking Manny if I can take his pack. I am already carrying four 1.5 liter bottles of water and my Nalgene bottle. I finally wrestle two waters from him and now have six in my pack. He is struggling and I am now beginning to realize we are slowing down to accommodate those who are not able to keep pace. I begin to worry that we might not make our objective.

By 8 am our pace has slowed to a crawl because Manny is having trouble, and I am again after his pack. He is stubborn. He thinks that if he can't make it, he will just turn around and go back. Alone. Amid the heat and humidity, the snakes, and the unexploded ordinance. The absurdity of that is mind-boggling. This is not a Sunday walk in the park. There are dangers everywhere.

10 am: Stan, Don and Sarge are okay, but Sarge is struggling a bit. The heavy clothes he has on are thoroughly soaked. We have covered perhaps a quarter of our distance to the top and we are going very slow. If we spend the night on the mountain we would cause a nasty little political incident and besides, we brought nothing to sleep on/in and the snake and unexploded ordinance

situation would be just too dangerous. Especially up there. I take the last bottle out of Manny's pack. He's not happy but I don't care. I'm angry and I know that anger is from anxiety about our ability to finish this task as a team. I now have seven bottles which present me with an odd sort of sloshing weight in my back pack. John Olsen takes Manny's pack and says he will carry it. As I talk with Manny he does not look at me.

Finally, at 10:30am, I talk with Major Carey and John Olsen about my concern for Manuel's condition. I tell Manuel that he should go back, that I can't let him go any further. Don says he doesn't think he can continue and volunteers to go back with Manny. Tom Gainer also accepts going back to assist Manny. Stan is wavering. He's already lost a lot of fluid. We are drinking water but the electrolytes we are losing at a rapid pace is putting people in danger.

This is not a good situation. In fact, it has real potential to be very bad. Not everyone in the group has the physical conditioning to make our goal. Perhaps 4 of us can. We have a long discussion about getting the coordinates precise and whether we split up the party. GPS is not working like we had hoped. We are alone in the jungle mountain region on the Lao/Vietnam border. There is no authority here but ourselves. Ngoc and our guide want to go on, knowing this is our only shot at making the hill. It is now obvious to us all that we can't come back on another day to do this. John also wants to go on as does Mike, Capt. Crowell and myself. But I am in a difficult position. How do I go on with the most able group and leave those who are beginning to succumb to the heat and humidity behind to return? The elements are so oppressive already. At this point I'm not sure Manny can even get back. We have no cell phone contact, we cannot get a vehicle up here and we cannot hire a helicopter. I am so Goddamned angry I could spit.

Major Carey and Captain Crowell finally decide that we will all turn around and go back. Mike says that 42 years ago he did not have a choice. This time he does, and he is not going to lose another man to this hill. I am fuming inside but trying to keep my composure. Gary Crowell sees right through me and knows that I want to continue on, even alone if I have to, and he calms me down by saying simply: "Unit loyalty, Doc: You can't buy it and we need you." Only about 8 miles into our quest, we now will do the 8 miles back. Adding insult to our situation, we remain unsure of the exact location of our hill. We believe we're only about three miles from the stream bed which is just a short distance to the base of 362. If we can find the stream bed, we'll find the hill. So close to our goals.

As everyone begins to head back down toward the road, I take a few more steps on the path leading upward and get a last, long look up the trail. I feel that these mountains no longer own me. I am here, on the slopes, ready to challenge it. I want to bare my chest and proclaim it. I am so close. I can feel the hilltop calling to me. It's like a magnet, pulling me, urging me to get closer, to be enveloped by the arms of its ghosts. I have this bizarre sense that there is something waiting for me up there that I can finally claim as my own or maybe something that will completely consume me once and for all. Perhaps it's a different kind of power. Perhaps it's my lost dignity that I feel calling to me. Whatever it is, it is strong and I can feel the earth trembling under my feet. For now however, I must turn back and help my mates get safely down this trail. Each and every one of us, in our own way, deals with the monster that lives on that hill and we are all here for a reckoning. Take us and be done with us, or let us bury you.

Unfortunately, our reckoning will have to come another day. I feel more cheated than anything else. Certainly, it was not the hill that defeated us today.

As we start out again, Stan begins to get sick and vomits several times. Everyone gets some of the salt tablets that John brought. Sarge is hangin' in pretty good but he looks shaky to me. We are stopping about every 3 minutes for Manuel to catch his breath. I am scared, deeply worried about him. His color is not good and I feel he may go into cardiac arrest. I ask the group for a 15 minute rest and get Manny to a small patch of shade. Heat and humidity continue to rise. I now start considering the negative possibilities and begin thinking of how to put a travois together and who I might enlist to help me pull it should Stan or Manny need it.

Finally we push on and I am running back and forth between Manny and Stan who is showing symptoms of heat stroke. Manny continues to appear dissociated from us all. Eberle is beginning to lag. Tom Gainer drops back to see if he can help. I am realizing we've made a big mistake and I am feeling guilty. I feel responsible for us not being well prepared to do this. As deeply disappointing as it is, the best thing at this point is to get everyone home in one piece and upright. I have to decide who I stick closest to, Manny or Stan. Mike has given me free reign to dictate pace and when to stop and start.

I'm walking mostly with Stan now; I have the back of his belt in my grasp, walking, holding him up as he is basically staggering. We stop again so that he can vomit. I'm amazed at his stamina and wonder how he can continue like this. Manuel seems to be recovering a bit but still needs to stop every few minutes. We finally convince Stan that he should not continue to carry the heavy marble plaque that

we intended to plant on the hill. I take it from his pack and
Gary Campbell asks me to let him carry it. Stan is white
as a sheet and soaking wet. At least he is still sweating. If
that stops he will be in dire straits. I fan him and pour
water over him each time we stop. I can waste my water
now. It is an agonizingly slow walk back in rising
temperatures. No matter where the path leads, everything
radiates heat. Not even the Elephant grass offers respite.
After many stops, Tom is exhausted but still volunteers to
take Manny's pack from John, and John takes the heavy
plaque from Gary. Major Carey discovers how much water
I'm carrying and takes two bottles out of my pack to
lighten my load.

Finally, we spot the road and soon after, the bus. Private
Holt, who stayed back with the bus, says in all honesty that
he was very worried. He did not expect us all to make it
back. He is a happy man and greets us like long lost
friends. Eberle cannot take his pack off and needs help
getting aboard. Stan is going to be OK but he's weak as a
kitten, as is Sarge, who came through better than I
expected. It appears that Manuel will be okay as long as he
doesn't do anything exertional. We are all in a kind of
daze, emotionally spent. There is very little talking on the
ride back toward the campgrounds.

Instead of spending another night outside of the tribal
village we decide to go back to DongHa. Don is getting
sicker by the minute and I'm wondering if he drank out of
one of the streams we crossed. He is vomiting far
too frequently. More than likely however, he is
hyponatremic and needs a good dose of electrolytes.

We break camp and pack our gear quickly. We have time
for only a short goodbye to the mountain tribe who so
graciously allowed our refuge in their area. On our way

back to the highway we decide that we do not want to take the stones back to America with us, so we stop and bury them in a field at the base of The Rockpile. Each of us take turns digging the grave site. This is not altogether unfitting. This is the spot we were extracted from by helicopter those many long years ago after our devastating fight. This is where we got our last glimpse of an area none of us ever wanted to come back to, let alone remember. Private Holt has reclaimed the large, marble memorial plaque but none of us ask what he has done with it.

We all gather around the makeshift grave and each of us has a few of the stones to place one at a time as we read the names off. I have a very hard time keeping my emotions in check when I place Frank's stone in this shallow grave.

This is not how I wanted it to be. Not on July 24, 1966, and not on May 4, 2008.

doug

Chapter 17
Markets and Musings

The billboards change the farther north one gets. We see lots of huge billboards with the VN star and the hammer and sickle of Russia and pictures of workers in hard hats looking off to the horizon and always with Uncle Ho's smiling face in the upper corner.

This far north the scars of war are deep. There is a different kind of feeling when we walk the streets and enter local restaurants. I feel a slight tension in the air. In the far south, SaiGon area, Americans and Europeans are more common. Here what they see mostly is American veterans looking to heal old wounds, many of whom probably stay to themselves, see the country from bus windows and continue to harbor suspicions of the locals.

Don spent the entire day in bed yesterday, vomiting frequently, but so far no diarrhea. He is urinating often enough and his pulse is strong. I'm pretty convinced he has hyponatremia, although some sort of gastroenteritis remains high on my list. I try to get him to drink some soup but he won't. He wants American wheat bread. Ngoc took me to the city hospital the night before and we tried to get some electrolyte tablets or vitamins from the pharmacy there, but we had no luck.

The group is off to see Khe Sahn and the tunnels today. I am staying behind to be with Don. Major Carey and Ngoc also stay behind. While Don stays in bed, the three of us have lunch together and Ngoc lets her hair down for the first time and talks a bit about her personal life. She has a husband and a 2 year old girl back in Hanoi. She misses them dearly. She will leave us tonight for home, a 12 hour train ride. She is such a wonderful person-so dedicated and such a hard worker. She is what Vietnam is about, beautiful, dedicated people. Every dictionary in the world should have her picture under Tour Guide. Just a remarkable person.

Earlier in the morning the 3 of us walk into DongHa (the hotel is at city edge) to the market. I want to get some bananas for Don. It is a huge open air market. Just everything. Soup to nuts. There are cosmetics, t-shirts, men's and women's clothing, nuts and bolts, large and small appliances from Thailand, thousands and thousands of shoes/sandals. The food market is massive, so many dried herbs for all sorts of ailments and cooking. I pinch them all and smell my fingers. The women point at me, talking, nodding their heads. I buy 3 large pieces of cinnamon and a bag of local black peppercorns for which DongHa is known. I know my friend John, back home, will love some of this. Still, no where can I find cigars, only cigarettes and Phillies. On the way out I buy some bananas for Don.

I wave and talk to everyone I see. They all respond. So many wonderful smiles. Mike says I am the official welcome wagon. These people are just remarkable. In few places have I experienced such complete and open kindness and generosity. There is not a cynic among them. The Vietnamese culture does not allow for suspicion or secrecy. The lives of the people are open books. They believe in family and spirits and they are deeply rooted, connected spiritually not only to all of the relatives that came before them but they also pray for those not yet born. Their future. There is good reason to envy this culture.

The market has pigs being slaughtered, fish gut soup, live and dead squid and very small crabs. I can't figure out what they do with these tiny hard shelled crabs. Every one beckons us to buy their wares. I wish I could take the whole market home with me. The smells are so intense. Pungent, sweet, acrid and foul. Very foul in some corners. I breath as deeply as my lungs allow, wanting to remember it all.

I realized on the walk to the market that I didn't put on enough sun screen this morning and the 3 kilometer walk gave me a good burn. I ask Ngoc if we can taxi back and she and Mike agree to it.

Don is happy for the bananas and I tell him no more than 1 per hour. They are Vietnamese bananas, very small, very sweet. There is almost a citrus note on the palate. The banana trees are everywhere here and I so clearly remember eating them back in '66-'67. Pineapples as well. We would eat pineapples until the corners of our mouths bled from the spines cutting our lips and then laugh at each other for the bleeding. It sure did beat eating C-rations.

Don is doing much better now. He's had 3 bananas and he's no longer vomiting. His stomach still aches. Duh! He's got good color and has a strong pulse. I am no longer worried about him. He's a good ol' farm boy from Ohio and sure has some grit to him. I expect tomorrow he'll be slapping us all on the back and flashing that huge grin of his. I appreciate his clean, easy and simple approach to life. He's a decent man and I am glad he is my friend and that he's getting well.

I know we are leaving tomorrow for DaNang. For me, it signals the end of this tour. Some of the guys came with lots of luggage. I came with a backpack and a tooth brush. I had one thing only on my mind and it wasn't vacation. I don't want to leave, but DaNang has a certain excitement of its own and I'll be happy to be there and back out on the coast. I am no longer disappointed about our quest, and am happy we are all together, a unit again. We put our lives on the line for each other at one time in history and in our hearts we would do it again. I begin to realize how much I care for these guys and in an odd way how much they have stayed with me for all of these years. We have all gone on to widely disparate lives and experiences, but we are connected forever in a way few people could understand. They are the thread that holds my tattered soul. They are a solid piece of my foundation.

Hope I can get another missive off before we leave.
Love to you all,
Doug

Chapter 18
Kit Carson

Friday morning, May 9, 2008
8:10am.

By this time tomorrow we'll all be in Hong Kong boarding
for the flight to LAX. It's funny; I feel this combination of
emotions. I ache deeply for my wife and sons and they and
my friends feel just a gazillion miles away but it seems now
that I have been here for only a day or two and I do not
want to leave Ngoc, Thuong and my old Marine Corps
friends. How does one fit this much intensity, adversity
and adventure into the short time we have been here?
Wow! This will be very hard to relate with adequate
description.

On our way back through DaNang and Marble Mtn, it took
all I could muster to not buy a 4foot tall marble urn and
have it shipped home. It was downright beautiful.
Shipping was only $100. Perhaps I should have splurged.
Thuong would get it for me; send it too, if I asked. Hmmm,
I'm thinking I haven't told you about Thuong. What a great
man. I am told he was wounded somewhere between 8 and
12 times, including being hit with a slowly rotating
helicopter blade, which would answer for the huge scar on
his right shoulder. He was a Kit Carson Scout with the
South Vietnamese Rangers during the war years. I should
have written a chapter on him. I believe he and I made a
special bond these past 2 weeks and I am honored to call
him friend. He has asked me to call his brother who lives
in New Hampshire as well as another friend of his in
Washington who served with the 101st Airborne.

I have a few chapters written that I've not sent out and I'm starting to think that maybe I will organize them all and write a short story of this trip. There have been smells and sights and sounds I do not ever want to forget and so many little snapshots in my mind of funny and dangerous moments. We became a Marine unit again. It was like getting back on a bicycle. Mike at point, Gary at our 6, John 1st man up and me in the middle, always in the middle. They won't let me take any of the fun positions. I'm hoping it means they like me.

By next week I will be back to my boring, hum-drum life where nothing exciting happens. That ain't all bad. Sometimes you should be careful what you wish for. The world is a wild and wooly place and hum-drum has its part.

Be well,
doug

Chapter 19
SaiGon

The Southern Monsoon rain storms are starting here. The southern monsoon season runs from May to September and the country is dominated by south to southeast winds off the South China Sea and Gulf of Tonkin. From October to April the north monsoon winds dominate, in the opposite direction. These monsoon winds happen at opposite ends of the calendar with only a short break in between. It's the south monsoons that bring most of the rain. Torrential rains occur with the typhoons that move in from the South China Sea. I can remember winds so strong it rained sideways for days on end in the central highlands or where ever the heck we were. We always used to joke about that, knowing no one back home would believe us, but it's true.

For now however, here in SaiGon, the clouds gather in the early afternoon and there is a soft rain for just an hour or two. It falls from the sky in tiny drops and so softly you almost don't know you're getting wet. It is the gentlest rain I have ever experienced. I know the winds and heavier rains will soon come, but today's rain, so soft and comforting, is easy and welcomed, like an old friend.

doug

Chapter 20
A Vietnamese Wife

This evening, John, Mike and I walk down to the Rex Hotel to have dinner at the roof top Garden Restaurant. We all order Vietnamese food. John and Mike get some beer, I settle for some red wine. We are enjoying the ambiance and each other's company. After dinner, I get up to use the men's room and on the way have a brief conversation with a young Chinese gentleman who is in SaiGon working for some sort of supply company. When I return to our table at the Garden Restaurant, I notice that John has changed seats. He originally was sitting on my right and Mike in the chair directly in front of me. Now however, John is across the table on Mike's left and the seat on my right is open. We order another round of drinks and just after they are brought a Vietnamese woman who looks to be about 45 years old comes to our table and sits down next to me. She immediately turns toward me in the seat and engages me in conversation, asking what part of America I am from and if I have a job. Mike and John are not taking part in the discussion. It doesn't take long before the woman has her hand on my leg, above my knee. I very carefully take her hand off and put it back in her lap. She doesn't wait even 5 seconds before she has her hand on my thigh again, only this time slightly higher up. Again I take her hand and move it back to her lap. I am thinking that if she is a prostitute, she is a little old to be working the Rex and she certainly is not getting the message that I am not interested. I have to forcibly remove her hand several more times during the conversation. Finally, as I turn to Mike and John to express my exasperation, they both have ear to ear grins. I pause and look back at the woman who says, "You want Vietnamese wife. I make very good wife for you." I look back at Mike and John again and they begin laughing hysterically. I suddenly realize they must have told someone I was looking for a wife to bring back to America. The joke was on me. We all got a good kick out of it and the woman finally got the message that my friends were playing a prank on me. She appears to take it well and bids us good bye. Soon after, the three of us walk back to our hotel to get some sleep.

Be well,
doug

Chapter 21
Hearts and Markets

The Ben Thanh Market in Saigon is the central market and it's enormous. Like all markets in Vietnam it has anything you could think of. I mean that. It's pretty remarkable that you can buy live fish, car parts and a TV at the same market. Past the silks, the art, the shoes, women's wear and cosmetics, the cookware, the radios and TVs and past the large, central eating area which has its own unique smells, I head for the fresh caught/harvested whatever. Meats, fish, vegetables, fruit. Dragon fruit has an incredibly delicate taste, wild colors and conformation, and pure white flesh speckled with many tiny black seeds, making it very appealing. Asian pears are so light, crisp and refreshing. They are like a drink of cool, sweet water.

There are squid of all sizes, large and small hard shell crabs, soft shelled crabs that remind me of Baltimore, and live frogs. I see octopus today. Prawns from 2-3 inches up to 8-10 inches. Small tuna, mackerel, catfish, many eels and so many other fish I don't recognize. There are pigs ears, pig brains and pig tails. All sorts of animal parts. Again, the smells are intense and swirling everywhere. I walk the aisles twice to look at everything, not wanting to miss something I've never seen before, trying to figure out ways I can take some of this home with me.

At the Majestic Hotel I can get a bottle of water for about $4, U.S. At the Ban Thanh market I can get the same bottle for 50 cents. I buy two of them. By the time I walk back to the hotel I am beat. Long walks in this heat and humidity are draining.

On our last night in SaiGon we all come together for a very nice meal at the roof top grill/restaurant at The Majestic Hotel. I order what appears to be some good wine and get no takers on sharing. The rest of the guys are having beer or mixed drinks. I have a couple of cigars from DaNang left in my pocket and I am content to have a long night of relaxing with wine and great smoke right here on the roof top overlooking the Saigon River and reflecting on these past two weeks. I know I am being redundant, but it has been just amazing.

SaiGon is changing and growing in many ways. The traffic situation is downright ugly. Only a few streets have stop lights and perhaps half the drivers obey them. No one signals. Not everyone stays to right or left unless on a boulevard and as a pedestrian you will never get across the road if you are not willing to step in front of a moving vehicle and force them to stop or go around you. No place for the infirm or wimps.

I cannot remember being this relaxed. I'm beginning to think the mission was well served after all, despite not making the hill. There has been an ache deep in my heart for so long. It took many years to come to terms with it and accept its presence. I used to peek at it now and then and I would talk to it occasionally, but always at arms' length and I spent many unproductive years trying to drown it with drugs and alcohol. I know the power and depth of the creature that lives there and I have learned to treat it with respect. I feel that now I have robbed it of a significant part of its power on this trip and it no longer has such command over me. I know for sure that coming here was the right thing to do. I hope to come home a better person.

This will be my last note until I get home and organize my papers. I will try to put together something organized and readable.

Can't wait to see you all again.

Be well,
Doug

Chapter 22
Home

May 11, 2008

With all its rushing demands and exacting schedules, home seems distantly familiar. I am hesitant to be drawn back into this part of my world. Reluctant to let go of the magic and emotion that has enveloped me these past two weeks. Not wanting to leave the camaraderie of battle mates made so long ago and now renewed. I want to close myself off, pour my emotions out and bathe in them. I am leaving something dear behind and I am sad. At the same time, I have recovered something long lost and I want to cherish it. Rediscover it. Welcome it.

My wife, my son and my friends have created a 6' x 20' foot "Welcome Home Vietnam Veteran" sign plastered over the front of our garage. I am moved to tears. This truly is a fitting bookend to the other life that existed in me from that first venture into Vietnam. A real welcome home after so long. It is heartfelt and accepted. My world has surely changed. No fanfare. No explosive emotions or hand wringing. My monster is beginning to fade. It has been a double edged sword for me all my life. Haunting me by night, driving me to perfection by day, always telling me I am not good enough. I am learning how to bid it farewell. I am learning how to be in control. I feel a final tether letting go.

Yes, after 42 years, I am home from Vietnam. Finally.

Chapter 23
Are We Done Yet?

I contacted Thuong's brother in New Hampshire. His wife was so funny, not speaking much English but excited to hear of our adventure. His daughter was effusive in her appreciation, and Anh, so much like his brother: Quiet, humble, but with a depth that reached through the phone lines and announced its presence. He is a proud factory worker, successfully integrating his family here in America. What wonderful people this family and these Vietnamese are. I am honored to know them.

The thing that sticks in my mind however, is that in the airport in L.A., as everyone collected their luggage and began heading off to their connecting flights for home, John Olsen, Gary Crowell and I had a moment when we were standing close together looking at each other in silence for about 10 seconds and we each said quietly, nearly in unison: "We have to go back."

A Trip Forward into the Past
Part Two

One More Try

Docs Howell and Gregory 1967
In the rear with the gear

Chapter 1

Here it is January, 2009 and I have just made my flight reservations to return yet again to Vietnam and another attempt at Hill 362. Mike Carey and I will be the only ones going, which is an interesting turn of events considering my conversations with him last spring. We will again be using Ngoc Nguyen as our guide, along with her husband, Phong, who we did not get to meet last year. I do not know at this point what other guides she may be using. We have only two objectives here this year and they are to find the site northwest of the Cam Lo River at the eastern end of what the American's called Mutter's Ridge, our Hill 362, and the stream bed site of the ambush two days prior to our fight on the hill. Ngoc says she will again employ a local mountain guide to help us. John, Gary Crowell and the other guys from the last trip have commitments that don't allow their participation this time around. They will be missed. John Olsen, especially. He did so much of the initial work for this.

Our plan is to meet up in Hue and drive to DongHa in the Quang Tri Province, which will serve as our base of operations. Ngoc has arranged a type of Russian-style Jeep for our use in trying to find the easiest route to the base of the hill and the stream bed. We aim to find the stones and monument we buried at the foot of The Rock Pile last year, then find our hill 362, rebury the monuments on top, document it, and get out. Afterward, we will head back down to SaiGon for a day or two before heading home. Déjàvu. Personally, I would like the simplicity of a smaller town for my R & R. More flavor of the Vietnamese life, and cheaper. But it doesn't matter. Mike and I are not likely to spend a lot of money on touristy types of things and we can be comfortable anywhere.

It has been a struggle for me to figure out how to approach this trip. I have been in communication with many people I met on our last trip there. In particular, Virginia Lockett, the physical therapist from America who, along with her husband, sold everything they had and moved to DaNang and began carving out a place where physical rehabilitation for the Vietnamese was moving forward rather than just spinning its wheels. I thought for a while that perhaps I could come over and deliver some medical education lectures of the sort that I give at the local universities here in Michigan. As discussion of this proceeded however, I realized that my lecture repertoire might not be what the rehab docs need. So I decided that I should continue to work with Virginia in trying to develop some sort of liaison with a PT school in Detroit. Perhaps an exchange program could be worked out. Because of the dates already set for meeting up with Mike and Ngoc, I will have to fly in a day or two early so that I have a week day where I can shadow Virginia and hopefully meet some of the docs at both the rehab hospital and the main hospital downtown to discuss future possibilities, including possible lectures.

So, I guess you could say that I am serving two purposes this time. One is to find an easier and safer route to Hill 362 and the streambed for the possibility of future groups who might want to visit. If we are successful with that, we hope to serve as Ngoc's liaison for setting up group tours. There is a business end to that. Secondly, I am hoping to establish some lasting contact with Virginia, the therapists and the doctors at the main hospital in DaNang in hopes that I can return again, maybe several times and be part of their educational program. There too, is a business end.

In the meantime, as both missions are developing, it is giving me an extra two days in DaNang when I will have nothing scheduled. Let's see, can I visit the local market to pick up bags of spices to send home, take a scooter down the highway to the ancient city of Hoi An and perhaps buy some souvenirs, scoot out to Marble Mountain, then see if I can climb Monkey Mountain and still have time to lounge on China Beach before I have to get on up the road to Hue and my meeting with Mike and Ngoc? Oh, I also want to look up some ex-pats here and see what they are up to. That's a tall order for just two days. Well, I can only do what I can do. I will sleep when I get home.

I do plan to rent a scooter as soon as I can when I get into DaNang and ride it as much as possible before I attempt to drive it the 40 miles up the coast to the PhuBai/Hue airport and meet Mike and Ngoc. Actually, I'm kind of excited about that prospect. My purpose in renting a scooter quickly is both to get used to handling it (It's been 40 years since I had my Harley Sprint.), and to test out the traffic scene to get a sense of the safety of me driving up the coast. Virginia says she takes her scooter down to Hoi An all the time, so I'm not anticipating problems. But better safe than sorry and practice certainly helps. Who knows what will happen however, and I am prepared to take a local bus if necessary.

January 30, 2009

I need to schedule a short flight from HCMCity to DaNang on my arrival day. I want to fly up there right away without having to spend money staying in the big city my first night. Ngoc reserved a flight for me but urged me to find my own because she could not find anything cheap. I asked the agent who booked my flights from Detroit to HCMCity what she could do and she also said it would be very expensive, around $150 U.S. My friend Auggie suggested that I try the online web site for JetStar Airlines. I did, and found a flight for $30 U.S. I am quite relieved. Outbound from the U.S., I will have my butt in an airport chair or an airplane seat from 7:30pm, March 17th to 5pm March 19th, local times. I am so going to need to go for a run the next morning to get the kinks out. I am excited about the prospect of running on the streets of DaNang or perhaps on China Beach.

Since there will be only two of us, plus our guide(s) this time, I have been studying the topographical maps of the area we'll be trekking in. I want to be as much help with our navigation as I can. Looking at these maps, I'm pretty sure I have located our hill and where we started from on our last adventure. It will be interesting to see what that stream bed will look like 43 years after our first encounter there. I see now why we had such a difficult time on our last trip. The approach we took appears so very far from our goal. The topographical maps we have today are different from those of the '60's and figuring these landmark goals is not an easy task.

Ngoc has informed us that she and her husband are planning to scout the area, looking for road access to the foot of the mountain in February, after the monsoon storms. Mike and I are anxious to hear what they will find. We very much expect to be able to drive right to the foot of our hill, making the climb somewhat easy. I'm hoping also that we can find a way so that more of our troop can make it to the top and pay their respects to the souls of the men who lost their lives there.

Chapter 2

2 February, 2009

Flights are paid for. I will send Ngoc her guide fees this
weekend. All I need is to take my e-tickets with me and
have money for hotels in DaNang, food, drink and taxi
service from the airports. I know that this time around I
am not interested in buying anything except for spices and I
intend to mail them home from DaNang so that I will have
room in my pack for any unexpected finds.

I can't shake this nagging bit of anxiety about this trip. I
don't know what it is, but it is bugging me. I'm trying to
deal with it realistically, telling myself to stay aware of the
dangers of snakes and UXO's, don't get foolish in the
cities, don't try to be superman on the mountain. Just do
the deal and get home.

4 February

The topo maps of the CamLo area arrived yesterday. Two
sets. One for Mike and me, one for Ngoc. Still waiting on
the Visa. I sent Ngoc her fee. Starting to put things
together. I'll gather up my clothes this weekend, see what
I've got. What I need. Mike will have a compass. I'll
have the maps. We should be able to find a road, dirt track,
path or something that gets us pretty close. We have lots of
days scheduled to look for suitable approaches. Plenty of
time to do a thorough job. I hope we can figure out how to
use John's GPS.

Chapter 3
May I have Your Ticket, Please

17 March 2009

The travel agent I used is in San Diego and specializes in Pacific Rim travel, primarily for Korean and Taiwanese areas. She was wonderful and she talked me into upgrading my seat class each way. This would give me a larger seat, a personal TV and larger menu choice.

Flights from Detroit to Seattle and Seattle to Taipei were uneventful. It is about 14 hours over the Pacific to Taipei, and like last year, I watched a lot of movies, read as much as I could and napped in between. The upgraded seat was a good idea. The extra leg room alone was well worth the price.

While in the Taipei airport waiting for my flight to SaiGon, I heard my seat number being called over the speaker. A little unnerving for sure, because it was obvious the plane was going to be loaded to the gills. I approached the attendants at the flight counter and was asked for my ticket, which I promptly gave to them. The attendant just as promptly tore it in half. I'm sure my eyes got as big a saucers and my jaw dropped to my chest. The Eva Air representative looked at me, smiled and very casually said: "No problem, you have new seat." He then handed me a ticket upgraded to a Business Class seating. I did not ask why. Fully reclining seats, real napkins, real silverware, multiple food choices, and multiple wine choices. I couldn't believe my luck. I had never flown anything but Economy class my entire life. I started out with a glass of Sherry before dinner and had a glass of champagne with the first course, which was a pate and then had a few glasses of Bordeaux with the entrée. It was an excellent meal.

Apparently, the jet from Taipei to HCMC did not have the same class seating as the flight over the ocean, so they had to either drop me down to the lower level Economy class or up to Business Class. What fun.

Before the flight and before getting my new seating assignment, while waiting in the Taipei airport, I happened to meet Rita, a very young 70 year old who was on her way to visit her son in Saigon. We chatted for quite a while then parted ways. When I took my bumped up Business Class seat on the flight to Vietnam, Rita was sitting next to me. She too had been bumped up to Business Class. We had an extremely good time, talking about wines and foods and traveling. She was a thoroughly delightful lady. She has a son in Saigon who is a school teacher and a son in Dubai who is a pilot. I think she said he flies for United Air Lines. She is so proud of both of them and she travels often to see them, though there are times when she wishes they lived closer to home. She lives in Seattle, was born in England, and seems quite proper. She told me she would be heading out to Dubai in the next month or two and I asked if it were any trouble to send some saffron back to the states. She agreed to send me some and said it would be no trouble at all.

Finally at the SaiGon airport, waiting for what seemed forever at the carousel for our luggage. Rita and I were two of very few remaining before our bags finally came out. I was getting extremely nervous because I had left a good deal of my money in my bag. Not smart, for sure. We were both a bit anxious for a while. When our bags finally arrived on the carousel, the last ones out and nearly simultaneously, I immediately took my money out and put it in a secure pocket. Whew!!

Then it was through customs quite easily and on to the JetStar and local flights area for my final leg up to DaNang. I said goodbye to Rita and as I walked out of the international terminal, looking for the local flights, a cabbie approached and when I asked him how far the local terminal was, he said he would drive me for only $10 U.S. My dismissal of him came just short of spitting on his shoes. He got my point. I'm probably lucky that I don't know any Vietnamese swear words. Finally, I found someone to point me in the right direction. I ask some more directions and find that the local terminal is right next to the international one and it took me only about 5 minutes to walk the distance between them. And he wanted to charge me $10 U.S. for the cab ride?

So, on to a JetStar flight to DaNang. Talk about small seats!! It's a good thing my flight was for only an hour. My knees were in my face the whole way. I slept as best I could. By this time, I am travel weary.

Be well,
doug

Chapter 4
DaNang Redux

19 March, 2009

We landed at DaNang about 5:30pm. I walked out of the terminal to get my bearings and to decide what to do. It has been a very long day of travel. A couple of Europeans asked me if I was continuing on down to Hoi An. I think they were looking to pool resources. I told them I was staying in DaNang, and I decided to take a taxi into town and go directly to the Bamboo Green Riverside Hotel. I had not made reservations. The hotel is right on the Han River, or *Song Han* in Vietnamese. A beautiful spot. They didn't have a room with a river view for my first night but assured me that I would have one for the rest of my stay. I was told I would not be charged the higher rate for the room with a view and balcony to compensate for not having one on my arrival. The desk man was quite accommodating, though I don't think I saw him smile the entire 3 days I was there.

As soon as I could wash my hands and face and brush my teeth, I got a taxi over the river to Virginia's house for dinner. It was exciting to be there and meet her eclectic little group. The house is on a main street on the east side of town, near the beaches and amid many local shops. She is only a few feet down from Tam Ky's Surf and burger shop. Like so many Vietnamese houses, there is no real front wall. It is all open, and passing by one can see the large front rooms on any and all floors of the house. Another small example of this open society. Usually, there is a moveable iron fence of some sort that can extend across the front when no one is home. Her husband Dave, her adopted Vietnamese son, Kim, along with Trong and Phuong were there. Trong cooked a wonderful traditional meal for us all but once we sat down to eat I almost immediately fell asleep nearly falling over in the chair in the process. The extended travel time and jet lag had caught up to me. I apologized deeply and Virginia gave me a lift home on her scooter. I hung on for dear life all the way back to the hotel, thinking I was going to fall asleep and fall off the back of the scooter and die or be run over on my first night in country. On the way, she gave some pointers on the city's geography, and I promised to get back to her place early the next morning. I was completely beat and once back in my hotel room slept very soundly. I'm anxious to experience the work at both hospitals with Virginia, see Hein and the folks at The Furama, Tam, an ex-pat by the name of Bill Erving if I can find him, and to explore the city. I felt happy to be back in DaNang.

20 March, 2009

The next day I had breakfast at the hotel. They put on a large spread of local cuisine and while I could not recognize everything, it all tasted great except for that one thing that was gritty and tough. A mystery food. After breakfast I hired a *xe om* (motorcycle taxi) back to Virginia's and spent the day with her. We visited her Rehab hospital and the Main Hospital C in downtown DaNang. It was an interesting day, but it became apparent that I would have very little to offer her or these hospitals. However, they were appreciative of the few physical therapy tools I did bring to them. The neurological rehab hospital is a bare bones operation. Virginia is an excellent therapist and is doing good work there. She is Type A all the way. A take charge person. It did not take long to realize that she has had to be that way. She has taken on a huge task here and it's obvious she is doing good work in a difficult and often resistant milieu. It's kind of like pushing a car to jump start it. Lots of strength and energy to get it moving, hoping to get it going fast enough for the engine to take over. I wish her all the best.

Friday night after dinner at Virginia's, I got a lift back across the Han to the hotel from a friend of Tam Ky and decided to hit the street for a beer somewhere. I walked about 8 blocks up river and found the Bamboo Café which I heard was a hangout for ex-pats. Amazingly, I found Bill Ervin at that very café and met a few other Americans there. Suel Jones and Don Blakely are two guys who work for the Vietnam Friendship Village program and both have been living in HaNoi but recently moved to DaNang. Suel is a super guy and I took to him almost immediately. I have recently learned that he has finished writing a book: *Meeting the Enemy: A Marine Returns Home*. I can't wait to read it. Bill Ervin is quite laid back. It was obvious that they are well known at the Bamboo 2 Café and the wait staff was extremely friendly with all of us. Don is quiet and reserved, a bit harder to read. But it was very comfortable sitting and talking with them. We had an enjoyable evening and about 11pm I wandered back to my hotel with promises to meet up tomorrow for a lunch on the beach.

21 March, 2009, Saturday morning

I took another *xe om* over the river to Tam's Pub. I wanted to rent a scooter from Tam for myself so that I did not have to depend on any one for transportation. Tam is a great person and she remembered our whole group from last year. I shared a cup of coffee with her and we talked for quite a spell about how she grew up on and around U.S. military bases during the American war and her continued connections with various ex-pats and visiting vets looking for some sort of closure for their war experiences.

I was a bit anxious about renting a motorcycle. It has been nearly 40 years since I'd been on one. So I thought I would just ride it around the block a couple of times to get used to it. Well, as it turned out, I drove it straight down to the beach, took a right turn onto the highway, put 3 liters of petrol in the tank and continued down the highway toward the Marble Mountains and Hoi Anh. I decided I would climb Marble Mountain and see its sights. My last duty in Vietnam back in 1967 was with the 3rd Battalion 1st Marines just outside of these Marble Mountains, but I never had the opportunity to see them close up or to climb around on them.

On my way, I stopped at The Furama Resort to see Hein. All of the young hostesses remembered our group from last year and asked how they were doing. I spotted Hein walking down a hallway carrying two buckets so I stepped out into the hall and when she saw me she dropped the buckets and ran up to me yelling "My doctor, my doctor!" and gave me a great, big hug. I couldn't believe she remembered me. They are all so gracious and have the brightest smiles. Hien was recently engaged and I am very happy for her. Big hugs all around and I had a large glass of plain orange juice. (Still learning the scooter, so no alcohol.) Hein scolded me for not bringing my wife along and made me promise to bring her back next time. I stayed for about 30 minutes, asking them all about their lives and telling them my plans, after which I got back on the scooter and continued on down to the Marble Mountains.

Chapter 5
Mountains of Marble

There are 5 mountains that comprise the Marble Mountain group. Collectively, they are known as *Ngu Hanh Son*, or Marble Mountains. They were named by one of the early kings of the Nguyen Dynasty (1802 – 1945) for the five essential elements of Vietnamese life: *Kim Son* – Metal; *Moc Son* – Wood; *Thuy Son* – Water; *Hoa Son* – Fire; *Tho Son* - Earth. These small mountains erupted straight up out of the sand and not a quarter of a mile from the Pacific Ocean on the beach. *Thuy Son* has the three peaks, the massive caves, and the steep stairways to the top where sits the beautiful *Tam Thai* pagoda, which in the past was used to worship both Hindu and Buddhist gods and now is dedicated to the Cham deities. This is the main tourist stop between DaNang and Hoi Anh. The Vietnam government has stopped the mining of marble in the main mountain. It is pretty depleted. All of the marble now comes from other areas. My fear is that someday there will be no marble left at all.

I began to question my physical condition when I first started climbing the mountain. The steps go nearly straight up and after a ways I was almost wheezing. Heart was pounding, legs were beginning to tighten up. I was just about ready to swear off all cigars and alcohol when I realized that I was taking these stairs about as fast as I could possibly go and that all I really needed to do was slow down. I wanted to do so many things on this day and I was in a hurry. There were many young people who were sitting down after climbing only 20 or 30 steps. It is a very steep climb.

Inside the main mountain, the Cave of the Heavens is spectacular. Pictures don't do it justice. Most of the cave entrances and the pagoda are near the top in a flattened area. There is a small, rugged trail that you can climb to reach the very peak. It is nearly straight up, but there is a makeshift, single hand rail. Finally on top, there is a tremendous view, looking out over the bright white coral sands of China Beach and into the deep blue-green of the South China Sea. I was so happy that I took the time and the opportunity to make the climb. The view was postcard perfect. I realized however that a similar trip to Monkey Mountain was probably not going to happen. I just did not have enough time.

On the way back I stopped at the beach just north of The Furama and had a late lunch with Suel, Don, Bill, Johnny V and his girlfriend (can't remember her name). We had squid, lobster, prawns, clams and steamed greens with garlic. From there we went to Bill's house near the beach. What a beautiful place. Brand spanking new. We talked for a long time. Very relaxed. Very content. I then rode back into the downtown area for a beer at the Bamboo Café and home/hotel by midnight.

22 March, 2009, Sunday

Sunday morning I went for a nice run along the river at about 6 am. As I crossed the road from the hotel to the river front I saw so many people out exercising and stretching. Most of them come out by 5am, long before the sun comes up. The paved areas are crowded with people of every ilk and age. Once the sun is over the horizon, the heat rises sharply and the crowds dwindle quickly. I was in awe of the number of people exercising all at once, all at the same place. Most were in groups, some small, some large. Many of these groups had some type of exercise uniforms and some even with flag bearers. Lots of the larger groups had an instructor or leader, so many of the participants were older people.

It is such a beautiful walkway along the Song Han. Colorful bricks and many, many large marble statues, a river walk any city in the world would be proud of.

I had another outstanding breakfast at the hotel, always starting with a steaming hot bowl of pho. Later that morning I rode over the river to Virginia's and she and I rode our scooters 25 Km south of DaNang to HoiAn, known as the ancient city. It is the place between HaNoi and SaiGon where most tourists go. There is an OLD VILLAGE there where the old ways of making syrups, clothing, harvesting rice and fish and many other aspects of life prior to machinery are shown. There are also many tailor shops and a large market. Many people buy Vietnamese silk and garments here. It is a very nice place, but too many tourists for me. At any rate, I bought some silk from a tailor and had her make me a bow tie, cummerbund and vest for my tuxedo. The material is bright red with dragon flies embroidered on. Seriously, you will burn your eyeballs out if you stare at it too long. It will certainly be a conversation piece at our next gala Christmas party back home. Virginia had work to do in Hoi An, so I rode my scooter back to DaNang alone and spent the remainder of Sunday tooling around, visiting Tam, Hien and the beach. Virginia said that she had a large gathering for dinner every Sunday night and to be sure to come over. I planned to motor over, drop my bike off at Tam's and walk down to Virginia and Dave's for dinner at 7. They are only a half a block apart. I hoped someone would give me a ride across the river to my hotel not too late so that I could grab a last beer at the Bamboo Café and say good bye to my other new found friends. Already, I was feeling a bit melancholy. I am enjoying myself in this city and there is so much more I want to see, do and explore.

Well, I went by Virginia's on my way to Tam's and there were no lights on and no one sitting in the front room. So I hung out at Tam's for a while and still, no one showed at Virginia's. Finally I called her and she and Dave and Phuong were having dinner at a small café across the street. Apparently, no one showed for her Sunday night dinner. I went over and had a beer and lau (hot pots on the table usually with beef, pork or seafood) with them. While there I saw probably the biggest rat I've ever seen in my life. So fat it waddled. One happy, sassy, DaNang city rat. It came out from the side of the café and down into a sewer opening in the alley. No one seemed to mind. I gave Virginia back the phone she so generously loaned me and said I needed to get back home. After dinner I got a ride back across the river by a local guy who hangs out at Tam's.

Chapter 6

23 March, 2009, Monday,

I packed my bag, ate a huge breakfast and spent some time
on the hotel's computer, not wanting to leave but anxious
to start the next phase of my journey. Also, I knew I was
going to see Thuong and Ngoc and to pick up Mike.
Happy and sad. I'm beginning to like DaNang very much,
and at the same time I am excited that the heart of the trip is
approaching. Ngoc was very nervous about me making my
own way up country to meet them in Dong Ha, despite my
eagerness to rent a scooter or take a local bus, so she
arranged for someone to pick me up. The driver showed up
at the hotel about noon and we were off to the PhuBai
Airport to pick up Mike. It is only about 40 miles but my
driver was so incredibly cautious I am sure that for the
longest time he was never went faster than about 20 mph.
We went over *Hai Vue* pass, which has spectacular views
of the central coast and of Da Nang and is lined with old
French embattlements, and then deeper into the mountains.
My view and my time on the coast was officially done. My
driver spoke almost no English and so I was alone with my
thoughts of the coming days and our quest for the hill. I
know I am physically ready for anything that the jungle
mountains can offer. My fears are for what lies on top and
what remains buried deep in my soul and in my memory.

While waiting at the small PhuBai airport, Thuong came
in, knowing I was there to pick up Mike. It was so great to
see him and he gave me a huge grin which told me that he
was also glad to see me. We talked about the past year,
how each of the guys are and about attempting to get to our
hill yet again this year. He agreed to get some tamarind,

Weasel coffee and pepper for me, but it was unlikely that we would get the chance to meet again. He looked good and I was content to get a few minutes with him. I gave him the Detroit shirt I bought for him and, when Mike arrived, he was given the military boots he had requested. I hope he was happy. Mike's flight arrived on time and he looked great as usual, like he was keeping himself in good shape.

With Mike now in from SaiGon, our driver headed the two of us out to DongHa to meet up with Ngoc and Phong. The drive would be about an hour and a half. The second part of my trip was now under way, and Mike and I spent the ride catching up on how life was treating us both.

Meeting Ngoc at the hotel in Dong Ha was very exciting. We were so happy to see her. Both her husband, Phong, and their daughter, Linh, were there as well. Linh is 2 ½, cute as a button, and very bright and energetic. She took to us immediately. Every time you point a camera at her she puts out her left hand with the peace symbol. She is learning English, French and Vietnamese languages. Her parents call her Kim, so we took to calling her that as well.

The 4 of us met in the evening over dinner at a local restaurant and planned out the next few days. Mike and I decide that we want to go up the mountain before looking for the stones and plaque. Retrospectively, I'm not sure why we made that decision, but we did. So the plan was that on Tuesday we would head on up the mountain, find 362 and get our bearings there, head down to the stream bed and try to find the that ambush site and then head back home. We planned to obtain the plaque and the stones on Wednesday, and if we found them early enough, head back to the hill and plant them. That left us with one day to play with in case things didn't go according to plan. That night Mike and I stayed up very late in our room and drank a bottle of Irish whiskey he brought with him from Guam. We had a great talk about, well, I'm not sure what. That single malt whiskey was very tasty.

Chapter 7
First Climb

24 March, Tuesday

Mike and I both woke up at the same time, about 5:30am; we showered quickly, put our packs for the trek through the jungle forest together, and then headed down to the lobby for breakfast. We were anxious to get moving toward the mountain. The 4 of us talked for a while about different routes, etc., and Ngoc told us she was going to stay behind with little Kim. I know deep down inside she very much wanted to be with us.

We took the ride out of town in our Isuzu to the far side of Chua Village, which is an older, well established village of displaced Lao mountain people at the base of the mountains. We left the driver, Ngoc and Kim at the car to return to the hotel and agreed on a time when we should be down from the mountain for them to return. So Mike, Phong and I, with the local guide Thach, who was with us last year, took off for the mountain. It was about 9:30am and already quite hot.

The walk was moderately difficult. Up and down many hills, steadily rising and crossing a half dozen streams. We are all absolutely sure of our destination and how to get there by the quickest route. Near one of the hilltops we found a small memorial for a local person who died there. I lit some of the incense that was left behind, said a small prayer for the unknown soul and we moved on. Some of the uphill climbs were quite steep and very rocky, probably a 5 mile hike. This would be very tough and slippery going in rainy weather. We easily found the crest to Hill 362 and the trek was not as physically demanding as we anticipated. I was very excited and wanted to scout the entire ridgeline to orient myself and find the saddle back. I ran down a ravine thinking that was the way to the ambush site. At the bottom was just a rivulet, which obviously was not what I was looking for. I realized, as I climbed back up again, that I must have gone down what was our right flank back on that day in '66. I remembered that flank as being less of a concern for us because the drop off was so steep I doubt any military unit would stage an attack from that direction. I went in search of shell casings or any metallic fragments I could find. Part of the crest had been flattened out by machine and I was digging along the edges, thinking I could find something. I suspect I looked a bit frantic because both Thach and Phong implored me to stop. They told me I would find nothing and any and every piece of metal was already taken from this hill top. I was on the verge of tears. I was finally on the hill. I was anxious and excited, wanting something for the guys back home, and as always, I was impatient. I kept thinking that there just had to be some remnants buried somewhere up there. A C-rat can, an empty magazine, a shell casing, something.

A small two room concrete house, measuring perhaps 12 x 15 feet, was built on the crest of the ridgeline, apparently for rangers who come once a year to check on the forest. It was in disrepair and appeared as though some one had a campfire in the middle of the floor. We ate lunch there in the dilapidated house and decided that on our next trip up, we would be more precise about a location for the memorial site. We were satisfied that we had found Hill 362 and there would be no mistaking how to get here. The feeling was a bit anticlimactic since we did not have the memorials and did not plan to do any ceremonies on this climb. It was now time to get down to the stream bed and find the other ambush site. This proved to be much more difficult.

24 March 2009
Searching for a path to the stream bed

Near the same area, 1966

Finding the streambed itself was easy enough, as there was a small path leading within 100 yards from it. Then we had to move off that small path and move through the brush. This is a bit more dangerous now because of UXO's and snakes. We were very careful to follow single file through this area. Phong took our point. We were on seldom used bits of old trails and for a while, making our own trail. Once on the stream bed the going was very rough. The bed is lined with huge, slick boulders and traversing down stream is tough going. The stream banks are quite steep on both sides and extremely thick with vines and brush. All of us slipped and fell more than once. I have a sore ankle, sore knees and a very sore right elbow. Mike twisted his right knee quite badly, though he did not tell us about it at the time. I later learned that he got his foot wedged between two boulders as he tried to take a long step, wrenching the knee and unable to extricate himself. He had to have Thach help him pull it out. Phong and I were about 30 yards ahead, further down the stream. There were many leeches and the vegetation hung very low off the low canopy over the stream. About half of our trek was in a bent over position.

As we headed down stream, Mike's job was to determine where we were and how far to go. I have almost no memory of the stream bed from 1966. It was Mike's third platoon that was ambushed. As they came down into the stream on that late afternoon in '66 looking for a clearing so that we could get resupply, Sgt. Brickey's first squad had the point and they began to see footprints and NVA clothing as well as other evidence of enemy presence. It appeared that some of them were bathing and eating in and near the stream before discovering the advancing Marines. Realizing there were enemies at this location, Mike reinforced the point before making further advancement. At that location, the stream came to an L that broke sharply to the right. The enemy had a machine gun set up about 30 yards from the sharp right turn with visual command of the entire stream bed and much of the right and left slopes. They also had riflemen positioned high up and closer to us on their right, which would be our left flank as we approached. Once they had that point team from Sgt. Brickey's first squad square in the machine gun sights, they opened fire. The banks of the stream bed were very steep and the vegetation thick with vines and dense underbrush so that flanking the stream, providing cover fire for those exposed in the stream and advancing on the gun position and the riflemen was nearly impossible, and the fire from that gun was extremely accurate. Nearly every Marine that tried advancement while in the beaten zone of the gun was killed or wounded. Two other squads were deployed, one on the left and one on the right flank to try to break up the ambush. Those Marines advancing on the flanks had to either squirm through that thick jungle underbrush or get into the stream bed with its uneven footing and complete exposure. Part of Sgt. Johnson's 3rd squad, including Don Eberle, Tom Gainer and John Olsen's fire team, had the unenviable task of attacking the left flank, temporarily exposing them to the raking fire of the machine gun. Those men were finally able to advance far enough on the enemy's right flank to break up the enemy positions. Once the gun's cover fire was neutralized, the enemy gun crew retreated, but not before we lost 8 KIA and 5 WIA from our 3rd platoon. By the time that fighting ended, it was dark and very difficult to see. Lt. Carey ordered some men to stay with the dead Marines while the rest of the platoon reformed and dug in for the night farther up out of that little stream valley.

Today, it took us about an hour and a half to find what Mike thought was the ambush spot. We stayed there for a while, looking it over both from upstream and down and he felt pretty confident that we had the right place. We all made mental markers of the area and took many photos. It was now time to find our way out and get back home. While no one was mentioning anything, I knew that I was about as sore as could be. I'm sure the others were too. The amount of times we twisted knees and ankles and fell into that stream was ridiculous. I had not yet come to hate it, but I already knew this stream bed was not a good place to be. Perhaps the ghosts of the past were making their own discomfort known to us.

The streambed 2009

For as far down stream as we had come, we knew that it couldn't be too far up the bank on the left to get back to our main trail, and sure enough, after pushing through the brush for about 15 minutes, we found a small seldom used trail. We did not hesitate at that little pathway. We took a right and very soon found the main trail. Another right onto that main trail and we were headed down the mountain toward the Chua Village. So, after a long and tiring day, we have identified our hill top and our stream bed sites. Again now we are trudging up and down over dry, rocky terrain steadily losing altitude. It was late afternoon and probably the hottest part of the day. About half way back, Mike began to have some trouble. He could no longer hide the fact that he was hurt. He was limping and I could tell he was in a lot of pain. I cut a staff from a young tree and gave that to him, which I think helped. But as time went on, it got worse. I was beginning to worry. I was feeling almost dissociated from reality and could not stop thinking of different war movies such as *Bridge Over The River Kwai*. We stopped often, every time we could find some shade or when we got to the top of each "next hill." I hung onto his pack a few times and asked if I could take it, but of course he refused. It was then that Mike informed me that he had had some recent surgeries. He is a Marine, perhaps the toughest I have ever known. I didn't expect that he would let me carry his pack, but I had to ask. There was no reason for us to hurry on this day, we had enough sunlight left to take our time and not push the pace beyond anyone's ability. As long as we took our time, I felt confident we could make it off the mountain. After a long and tiring day, we felt confident that we identified our hill top and our stream bed sites.

So our trip back turned into a pretty slow walk with frequent stops and as we neared the village, Phong began a quick step to get some water from the car that we hoped was waiting for us while Mike, Thach and I tried to keep a steady pace. It wasn't too long before Phong came back to meet us with lots of cold water. We knew then the car was close and we were greatly relieved.

105

We got back into the Isuzu and the driver had a cooler of cold Huda beer for us. That is good enough to make sore and tired men smile. Ngoc and Phong are taking good care of us. As we got through the village, on the east side, one of the local farmers had been collecting wood and had hundreds of chopped and trimmed young trees lying across the dirt road way. There was no way a car could pass so we all got out and started moving the trees off into the farmers' yard. It took us only about 15 minutes and we then had enough room to squeeze the car by without falling into the rice paddy and were on our way back to Dong Ha and our brand spanking new hotel.

Chapter 8

When we got back Ngoc and Kim greeted us like old friends. It was a very warm feeling and I couldn't help but think how easy it is to like these people so very much. Mike and I talked with them in the lobby for a while, and then I went up to our room, got my box of cigars and came back down. I found someone to sell me a bottle of wine and talked them into giving me a small, squat drinking glass instead of those off-sized wine goblets that come in hotel restaurants. Then I went out onto the gleaming white steps of the hotel and sat down off to one side, lit a cigar and poured myself a glass of wine. It was good to be in Dong Ha and it was very good to know we found our hill. The guys back home will be excited and pleased, I'm sure. I can't wait to tell them about it.

A young man, Duong, approached me and asked if he could sit and talk. I offered him a cigar, a drink of my wine and we talked for about 15 minutes. He was very friendly and my thought was that he just wanted to practice his English. He said he worked there at the hotel. He soon took off on his scooter and I was again left alone to my cigar, my wine and my contemplations of the days' events. Another man approached me and while he did not speak English, it appeared that he was interested in my cigars. I read him as unfriendly and did not offer him a cigar but did offer a drink of my wine as sort of a test. He declined my offer and left. He definitely did not give off friendly vibes.

About 45 minutes later, Duong came back on his scooter and asked if I would accompany him down the street. He said he would like to buy me a beer. Again, I thought he was a friendly sort and so I agreed. It was now late enough to be dark. I hopped on his scooter with him and we went about 6 blocks down the street to a tiny corner spot like so many in Vietnam. There was a sort of plastic cover about 5 feet high over the ubiquitous plastic sidewalk tables. The cover was tied to telephone pole guy lines because of a light rain at the time. Just a few small typical plastic tables and chairs with a food and beer stand by the curb. We talked about many things, sports, politics, and the hotel where he works. His friend, it turns out, is a chef at the hotel. They bought some food for us all to eat. I have no idea what it was and I was not very hungry but it tasted pretty good and I ate enough to be polite. They absolutely refused to let me pay for anything.

They have a great tradition there. When men go out to drink, they all put an ice cube in their glass, opening just one bottle and pouring for everyone. Then someone makes a toast, they all drink the glass down after which everyone shakes hands. Then they do it all over again. Each time. Every time. Even guys who go out all the time with each other. Soon, I told Duong I had to go. I was very tired. Again, they would not let me pay or accept any money from me at all. He gave me a ride back to the hotel where I found my cigars, my bottle of wine and my glass on the hotel steps exactly where I left them. Something that will happen almost every time when you are in Vietnam. If it does not belong to them, the Vietnamese do not take it. My wine and cigars could have stayed there all night and I would still find them there the next morning. What is not to like about that? Of course that can't be said for some of the neighborhoods in the larger cities.

Wednesday, 25 March 2009

Again, Mike and I were up about 5:30 and showered, dressed and ready for breakfast by 6. We took John's GPS and our maps and all headed out to the Rockpile to look for John's stones and Joe's plaque. Ngoc brought little Kim with us which made me happy. Mike is having a very hard time with his knee today. He can hardly get up once seated. He's in a lot of pain and he mentioned to me that he might have to beg off on the next trip up the hill, leaving me alone to find the saddle back and a suitable burial site. I am feeling very sluggish and tired today. I have no energy.

Joe Holt, who was with us on our search in 2008, had buried the plaque somewhere off the road near the Rockpile. For location and identification purposes, he took a bunch of photographs of the area where he put it. Prior to my return with Major Carey, Joe sent me copies of those photos in hopes that we'd be able to find that plaque. Thach (pronounced tek) and I looked at Joe's pictures and we took off down the road looking for the plaque. It was so easy to find. His description was enough. The pictures just made it even easier. As we dug it out, a few of the local workers from the quarry down the road were coming by and stopped to watch. When we pulled out the plaque we noticed something red underneath it. As we pulled the red thing out, we realized that it was a flag. Some years ago, Joe had been given a Vietnamese Liberation flag which had blood stains on it and he brought it with him on our trip and decided to bury it under our plaque. He didn't tell a soul. One of the locals who were watching told us that Joe was spotted last year burying these things and soon after we left they were dug up. Apparently, whoever dug it up was impressed enough with the plaque and flag that they reburied it at the same spot. I wonder if that would have been true had there been no Vietnamese flag.

The stones were another story. We spent six hours digging here and there for them and just couldn't find them. We had a GPS location, but that really gave us an area 10 to 20 meters to any side of the site, essentially a 40 meter diameter and we weren't even sure of that. Something was not right. We searched a very large area, finding nothing.

Eventually, we had to force Phong to stop digging and looking. He was just like a blood hound. It was too late now to go to 362. We'd never make it up there and back before night fall. So we went back to the hotel unsure of what to do on Thursday, our last day to get the mission accomplished.

While spending the afternoon back at the hotel we happen to meet a group involved with clearing mines and other UXO in the Quang Tri Provence area. We introduce ourselves to an American, Chuck Searcy, who explains some of their work and that they are associated with the Project RENEW teams who are largely responsible for searching out and clearing farm land from these war leftovers as well as assisting and supporting survivors and families of victims of accidental explosions. Hundreds of Vietnamese are killed and maimed each year because of these explosives. The team that is staying at the hotel is composed of a mixture of cultures, mostly Vietnamese and American and both Mike and I are struck by the intensity of their demeanor. True to my nature, I immediately want to join them and help in their search and clearing projects. Of course I cannot, but I find their work humanitarian and necessary. A great number of the UXO is in the form of the cluster bombs that we dropped in such large numbers during the war years. These types of bombs are engineered to explode before they hit the ground and spread shrapnel over a large area. I remember all too well my very first encounter with what such ordinance can do. During our first operation in Vietnam we took small arms fire from a hamlet and were pinned down for long enough to call in air support. Some or all of that support, I can't remember exactly, was in the form of cluster bombs. Once we felt that we could approach the hamlet safely, we found a young girl out in a field. She was perhaps 15, lying next to an older woman who was dead. The young girl had her left leg blown off just below the knee. She was bleeding badly. It appeared that she had crawled to a nearby pond and filled her conical hat with water and then crawled back to sit next to the older woman who turned out to be her grandmother. The young woman was crying, wailing loudly.

This young woman was the very first serious combat casualty I treated in Vietnam. I removed my belt and tied it around her leg as a tourniquet. As I treated her, there were several Marines who stood nearby so that I was not left alone while the rest of the company searched the Hamlet and nearby areas. We made a decision that we could not leave her in her current condition so we called for a helicopter to medivac her out. Once the chopper arrived and she realized we were going to put her on it, she grabbed onto me as tightly as she could and looked terrified. She knew only that the Americans were taking her away in a flying machine. She did not know why or where to. Once on the chopper she reached out at me with both arms, eyes as wide as could be, yelling in Vietnamese over the roar of the engine and rotating blades. She was so obviously pleading with me not to let them take her. She left with my belt still around her leg and I have never forgotten her nor have I ever forgotten the very desperate look in her eyes. Cluster bombs deliver devastating damage.

Chapter 9
Cool Nights Warm Days

This night Ngoc, Phong and Kim took us to a restaurant on the CamLo river. A beautiful outdoor place on the river's edge. We once again had much seafood, and beer that they put on ice for us. Kim of course was all over the place. It was nice to sit outside with so many other Vietnamese, enjoying the beautiful evening on the banks of the Cam Lo river. Everyone was laughing and having a good time. There were a few couples and several large groups of 8 to 12. March is a good time of year in this part of the country. The early monsoon season has ended It is still before the real heat of summer, and there are very few bugs. Cool nights and warm days. This is a very lovely and peaceful scene and I am so happy to be here with these friends. I am coming to think of Ngoc and Phong as more than just hired guides or acquaintances. They are friends. They care about us sincerely and I am beginning to care for them the same way. The Vietnamese are very open and giving. Little Kimmie acts as if she's known us forever. She calls me *bac sy, or bac si*, (doctor) and she calls Mike *onh*, (grandpa).

Chapter 10
Last Chance

Thursday, 26 March

At breakfast it seems like every one but me wants to go back to look for the stones. I am very concerned that this is our last day to place any memorial up on the hill and I am comfortable letting the stones rest right where they are. Wherever that is. Phong is adamant that he can get close to the spot this morning. He spent a great amount of time last night refiguring the data using Google Earth and more GPS figures. I made a request that we spend no more than one hour looking for the stones and after that we move on out to the hill to make our way up and plant the plaque. The Rock Pile is in the opposite direction of where we need to go to get to the Chua Village and Hill 362. Everyone agrees to the one hour time frame. Mike tells us that he cannot make the attempt up the hill and certainly not back into the stream bed on this day. That leaves only me from India Company to complete the mission. My anxiety begins to climb.

Once back out at the Rock Pile, Phong takes measurements from some trees and bushes before going off the dirt road, marks off a spot at the edge of the road, and walks into the brush. The road had been graded over at least once since last year, maybe several times, and was wider than we remembered it. About 15 minutes later he finds a spot that looks like it had been dug up previously, sticks the mattock in and strikes stone. We all look at each other and he begins digging quickly. It is our burial site from last year and all the stones are right there. I can't believe it. I really had given up hope on finding these stones. My respect for Phong continues to rise. He has a great grin on his face.

He is happy and proud, as he should be. He found a needle in a haystack.

We put all of the stones in a bag, put them into my pack and head back out toward the main road and the Chua Village. On the way we pass over the Cam Lo River and decide to wash the stones and document them. As we sit on the river's sandy shore, Mike washes them off in the water and I mark down on paper everyone's name and split them into two groups: One group for the stream bed and one for the hill top. Some local village people come out to see what we are up to, but soon enough we are back in the Isuzu and off to the Chua village and the path up the mountain.

After arriving on the west side of the village, Phong, Thach and I saddle up for the trip up the hill and now that we have the stones again we will go back down into the stream bed too. Kim has a hold of my hand just like she intends to go with us. She is so darn cute in her sun hat and bright yellow summer dress. We take some pictures and explain to Kim that she has to stay at the car with mom. She doesn't take it very well.

Phong carries the mattock, the machete and some water, Thach carries water and our lunches and I carry the stones and the plaque, as well as water, and what I call my superman mix (Gatorade powder). For the last time on this trip, perhaps the very last time ever, I head out for Hill 362 and the stream bed. I begin focusing just like I do before running a marathon. I do not focus on the work of getting up the hill or down around the stream. I envision only the placing of the memorials and arriving back at the village. My biggest concern now is not physical. I am worried that I am not worthy of this task. I know that I can do the job, but am I really the right person to be doing it? How could this happen, that I am the only one left to do this? With all the guilt that I have borne over all these years, how do I do this without saying "I'm sorry, it's only me" when I get up there and have to speak to those fallen Marines? My heroes. For one of the few times in my life, I am completely at a loss for what to say.

As we start, Phong leads, followed by Thach, then me at our six. We go around the first bend, lose sight of the Isuzu, the driver, Ngoc and Kim and we cross the first shallow, rocky stream on the other side of which begins the first set of small hills as we approach the larger ones. Perhaps twenty minutes into the hike Phuong stops and says we will take a break. We all drink some water and stand around for a few minutes. Finally, I tell Phuong that I don't want to take any more breaks unless we have to. I just want to get up quickly. It is not as hot today and I don't see a problem with hiking straight up. I consider all three of us strong enough to do the whole day without more than a quick lunch break and that is what I want. I'm not sure at all how far along the crest of 362 we will have to go before I feel comfortable planting the memorial and I surely don't know how long getting stuff placed at the streambed will take. I know we will be much farther up on the ridge where no people go. With all the snake holes we have seen these days, I am very aware of them up there in the thick brush. Not to mention the chance of stray armament. Today I'm wishing I had Stan's high top leather boots. We will be well off the trails. I think about the absurd irony of being hurt, possibly seriously, by some sort of explosion. This time, however, while I am very much aware of the dangers, I do not fear them. In fact, quite the opposite. I am here not just for the fallen Marines of my past, but for myself as well. I am here to put a stake through the heart of that fear and exorcise the monster that has ravaged my dreams for so many years. Snakes and UXO's cannot hold a candle to the power of that beast.

I set out in the lead on what I think is a good, brisk pace and about an hour into our hike I realize that I can't see the guides behind me anymore. We are more than half way to the base of the hill and I also realize that I have put myself into a typical workout trance. I am working hard and doing the mental imaging that takes my mind off the physical aspect of the work. Still though, I stop for a while, sit, and drink some Gatorade. Once I see Phuong and Thach, I wave to them, restart my pace and don't stop until I get to the crest of the hill where the small ranger station is located. I drop my pack and step around this small, concrete structure and look at the trees and dense brush in front of me, trying to envision the thin crest of this hill far out on the east end of Mutter's Ridge and how far it might go until the saddle back. Am I a hundred yards from it? Two hundred? Three?

As Phong and Thach arrive on the hill crest, I tell them that we should just start pushing through and try to stay on the crest until we hit the saddle back. We will have to concentrate on staying up on this broad crest while working our way through the brush which is about 8 feet tall, very thick and full of vines and who knows what else.

I have not mentioned the change of the landscape from when we were here in '66. It is so very different now. Because of the long history of wars and the embargo following the war with America, the country was in bad need of hard currency after 1975. It paid its war debt to Russia in oil from off the coast, and it cut vast tracts of timber for wood and pulp export and for furniture products. That, in combination with the extensive amount of Agent Orange, denuded huge areas of Vietnam's beautiful jungles. There is no longer a triple canopy jungle in many places. Since the late 1980's and early 1990's however, the country invested thousands of people to plant the gum trees that have now replaced many of those old, dense and beautiful jungles. Maybe in another 50-75 years it will morph back to a semblance of its former self.

Once again I am in the lead, pushing through this very thick brush. Again, it is the first and only time that I wish I had high top leather boots but I try not to think about snakes and bombs. And to think two years ago we imagined spending the night on this hill. How ridiculous. I am trying to use the machete, but it's almost useless. The vines are everywhere, from one inch off the ground to over head and they grab at everything that comes through. I just have to bull my way through this stuff and keep an eye on the ground before me, watching for snake holes or anything that does not look like it belongs to this terrain. After what seems to be two or three hundred yards, I feel like we are ever so slightly sliding off to the left. Phong says he will climb a tree to see where we are. The forest is very thick here. I tell him that he doesn't know what to look for. I will climb the tree. As I hoist myself up, I get to the lower set of main limbs and hang on, looking out over the brush. It takes me a while to get my bearings. I realize that we are only just a tad off the side of the crest and as I look North/Northeast I see that the brush and tree line take a distinctive dip and then rise again further down, right in front of me. Something about it doesn't quite register. There is a uniformity of the pale green color and conformation of the trees and underlying brush that does not excite any memory cells. It is a different type of jungle now. I must have stared at it for two minutes before I accept its significance. It's a saddle back depression in the topography. It can't be more than thirty yards. My heart

117

skips a beat and the hair on my neck is standing straight on end. A cold shiver runs through me. Is that really it? There's no one else here to confirm it. I believe I am on Hill 362 at the north east end of Mutter's Ridge. I know we are very near our battle site. Very near. What else could that be? I make my decision. We are at the end of the search. As I stare at this dip in the Ridge I say to the guides "We're here. Drop your packs." Now my anxiety really begins to rise. Where do I put the stones? Should I move down further? Should I be right in the saddle back? What is wrong with this spot right here? This spot would be closer to where we established our ragged and thin perimeter and spent those fateful two days. I decide to put the stones right here, thinking that I will put the guys inside of that perimeter, right where we would have wanted them to be on that night so long ago. Here we can guard them forever. My emotions are swirling making it hard to concentrate. I do not feel deserving of this moment, but I will do the best I can do. I owe my life to these men. Damn, I wish John and Mike were here. I wish they were all here. I have so many wishes at this moment.

We find a spot between a gum tree and a very large boulder that will be perfect for a burial site and we use the mattock to start digging. First me, then Phuong, then Thach. We all take part in preparing a square, deep hole. The roots are thick and tangled and it is a bit tough digging. Once the hole is about 12 – 16 inches deep, I ask Thach to use my camera and set it to video record. I begin to have a feeling of a very crowded hilltop, as though many people are looking over my shoulder trying to look down into the dug out earth. I take each stone out of the bag, read the names and place them in the ground. I save Frank's until next to last and then put Lt. Kopfler's stone on top of them all. I then place the plaque over the stones. With a short, silent prayer, I then start to cover them. Thach wonders if I am going to place the flag over the stones and I have to tell her that the American flag does not get buried. It is a slightly awkward moment. I finish covering the site and we mark the spot with the GPS and take video of the direction back to the Ranger shack. Hopefully, it is a spot that can be located again if necessary. In retrospect, I regret not having blazed the south side of the tree, not lingering a little longer at the site and not saying my prayer aloud for the recording and for the rest of the guys to hear at our reunion in the fall. Worse, I had a nicely prepared, simple eulogy I was going to read for the video that I thought everyone would appreciate and in the chaos of thoughts going through my head, I completely forgot about it. I was in over my head with emotion. I was burying those memorials for my fallen heroes, my brothers. But for me, the memorial was also for all of the Vietnamese we killed those two days, and there were so many of them. It was for the tragedy of war. And, finally, I was making my first attempt at burying the monster that has lived in my heart for so many years.

We pushed our way back to the house and the guides started preparing lunch. As they did, I reviewed the video, after which I broke down and started to cry. I left the house and walked to the south west crest of the hill. I am feeling relief, regret, sorrow, guilt and a very uneasy sense of accomplishment. I am trying to hold all the guys as close in my thoughts as possible. I feel so very much alone at this moment and give out a tremendous yell of angst. I compose myself as quickly as I can and walk back to the house. Thach immediately asks in a very matter of fact manner if I was ok now and if I could continue on. She is The Rock Lady. I didn't have much of an appetite and lunch was over with quickly. I very much wanted to get down to the stream bed and get this day over with as quickly as possible. I'm sure my anxiety was palpable.

119

Again, we headed down off the hill and at the bottom took a hard right down to the old trail we found earlier and then left again toward the stream bed. I know I am maintaining a wicked pace for my guides, but I can't help it. Something other than myself is pushing me forward. That first ambush spot is not hard to find now. We were just there two days ago and know the valley floor between these mountains a bit better.

We reach the stream and take another right to head up stream, looking for the site that Mike pointed out two days ago. I am actually nervous that I might not recognize the spot.

About two or three hundred yards up we come to an upside down L and I am sure this is it. I walk up stream and down and, again, I am certain. There are some huge boulders on the right as we head up stream and these will serve as good pictorial markers. They are unique in conformation. Phong and I pick a place that looks like it will not be too affected by monsoons or flooding. We clear out a spot behind a very large boulder. Still in water, which I think is necessary, but near enough to the edge that you don't have to stand in the stream to access it. I set the camera to video and hand it to Thach to record placing the stones and repeat the procedure from the hill top, reading each name before placing it in the hole. Again I pray that our fallen brothers rest in peace and I then placed a large boulder over the top. We took several pictures of the spot, including pictures up stream and down. It is midafternoon now, and time to go home. There is no more work to be done other than to get home in one piece. As we turn to head downstream to look for a way out of the stream bed, Thach calls our attention to what appears to be a small trail leading up on the left off the stream. It looks like perhaps an animal trail. Phuong immediately says, "I know this one. It will take us to another trail that will lead right to where the main path back to the village is." We shoot straight up off the streambed and sure enough, perhaps 50 yards up is a narrow trail but appears well trodden enough, and leads in the direction to the main path. The trail up off the stream bed must have been an animal trail down to the water. It was barely visible. I'm not sure I would have ever seen it, but it is perfect. Any UXO would have been tripped by animals heading down to the water, long ago. Phong now has a much better idea of how to lead people to the streambed burial site. He is meticulous in his notes and I have no doubt that tonight, long after every one is asleep, he will be drawing pictures and describing this little trail in his journal for future reference. He takes his job seriously and I can't say often enough about how lucky we are to have him, Ngoc and Thach as our primary guides.

Once again I take off on a brisk pace, heading back to the SUV and the Chua Village. This time, Phong and Thach stay with me. I am bursting with happiness, and occasionally skipping, almost running as we walk up and down these hills. It is readily apparent on my face. At one point I am skipping sideways up to the top of one of the hills and Phong says to me "You are very strong, bac si, very strong." I reply to him "This is emotion! I am just very happy because of what you have helped me do today" and I give them both a very strong hug. As we get close to the village we meet two Lao mountain women, both carrying old Chinese metal detectors. We stop and chat for a while and I get some great pictures of them. They tell us that they can make more money looking for metal up in the hills than they can in a year of farming. I can't help but wonder how many times they find unexploded ordinance and how many of them have died or lost limbs doing this kind of work. It occurs to me that if I had time, I would love to hire them and take them back up onto our hill and search for remnants of our time there in 1966. Perhaps if John gets to go back next year it is an idea he can entertain.

When we return to the SUV, the driver wants us to check for leeches before we get in. He keeps that car immaculate. I find about 10 of them on my feet and ankles and most of them come right off with a flick of the finger. They are so fat and swollen with my blood. Some are a little more stubborn. This is really a lot more leeches than I had the first time down in that stream and I can see now lots of little open sores all over my legs and feet where I must have had many more of these things who sated themselves, detached and once again began floating on the water awaiting the next victim. Thach shrieks with each leech that she flicks off and I realize that this is the first and only time I have seen any emotion at all from her other than her great smile. She doesn't like the little black creatures. I am strangely comforted by this. There is a soft spot to her after all. The driver again has a cooler of beer for us. Phong and Thach do not drink, but I am hot, tired, and deliriously happy, and I pull on the first one very quickly and then savor the cool taste of the next. On the way back I keep thanking all of them over and over. It's really beginning to hit me that I think the search is over, that we have finally completed the first and most difficult step in what may be a long process of having guys reconnect with the physical site of a battle that is etched deeply and painfully into the hearts and minds of the men of India Company.

Chapter 11
Bitter Sweet Food

When we pull up to the hotel and as I get out, a huge leech falls out of my shirt and onto the pristine white marble steps of the hotel and splatters blood over it. It makes for quite a scene. I am filthy dirty, soaked with sweat, caked with mud and buffalo cow dung and smelling pretty rank, I have dropped a huge leech on the pearl white steps of a brand spanking new down town Dong Ha hotel. I must have been a sight. And I am an American. Nice.

Mike comes down from the room and gives me a big hug and thanks for a job well done. I take some of the beer, buy another bottle of wine, and Mike and I head back up to our room. We sit on the floor and talk for an hour or two about the entire mission and how much we wish the other guys were with us. Most particularly John. He started this whole mission and he is sorely missed.

I am emotionally and physically spent. As I describe to Mike both of the burial sites and show him the pictures, I began to realize my hatred towards that stream bed. Despite some of the picturesque views of small water falls and pools and shady coves, it is an evil place. It was evil 43 years ago. It is evil still today. There is no way I would ever want to step foot in it again, unless to guide fellow Marines there to our burial site.

With my shoes off I notice that my feet are beginning to swell quite a bit. I tell Mike that I need to shower and clean up. I am sure we'll go out to dinner again tonight. There's never a bad time or place for great food, particularly seafood, in Vietnam.

Once in the shower I find yet two more leeches, both very fat and filled with my blood, one of them in my groin area and I start a more thorough inspection, including places that don't usually get that much attention.

We had another great meal that night. The restaurant has very large tanks full of snapper and other fish, crabs, lobsters, snails, shrimp, sea snakes, all kinds of live seafood. You get to pick out whatever you want and it is killed and cooked right then and there. Steamed, broiled, barbequed, whatever you want. While the food is great, the meal is kind of bitter sweet. We will be leaving the next day for HCMCity and I'm thinking that I might never see these people again. Little Kimmie sits next to me for a while, then back with her mom, then back with me and Mike. I want to take them all home with me. Most especially this smiling and energetic young girl who for all the world appears to have an unlimited future before her. I couldn't be happier for them all. These are very special people and very deserving of all good things. Phong is an incredible guide; fearless, determined and intuitive. I have such deep respect for him. Ngoc, a great guide in her own right, is Earth Mother. She is so loving and caring of everything around her. She makes us all feel comfortable and at home, no matter where we are or how difficult the situation. Mike and I again pay for dinner and we give Ngoc and Phong 2 million VN Dong ($100 US) as a tip for their service to us these past several days. It is not enough. No amount of money could be enough for what they have given us.

Chapter 12
Back to Civilization

March 27th

The next morning Mike and I are packed up and ready to go. While waiting for our driver we talk with Phuong and Ngoc about future trips and how Mike and I might partner up with them on tour groups. We bat around a few ideas. Slowly, Kim begins to realize that we are leaving and she starts to hang on me and Mike. We take a bunch of pictures. The driver arrives and Ngoc gives me a very warm kiss on my cheek and tells me they will miss me. I had tears in my eyes then and I have tears in my eyes now as I write this. Kim begins crying loudly as Mike and I get in the car to leave. I can still hear her: "Bac sy! Khong di, bac sy!" "Don't leave!" I blow her a kiss and make a silent promise that I will see her again, just as soon as I can. This family has found its way deep into my heart.

So we start the slow trip back down to the Hue/Phu Bai airport. It's about a 2 hour ride. Ngoc and Phong gave me a couple of kilos of black and white pepper from Khe Sanh which is considered some of the very best in the world and also bought me a shoulder bag to carry it in. They would not let me pay for it. The driver has also brought me pepper, imitation Weasel coffee and fresh tamarind from Thuong. As Vietnam becomes more and more open to a free market economy their access to better and newer agricultural information allows them to greatly increase the quality of their products. They are quickly making a name for themselves in the world market.

Chapter 13
Hue and The Imperial City

We have never had a chance to spend much time in Hue.
Last year, while driving though, we had a great lunch here,
but that was the extent of it. The Imperial City is here at
the center of town. Lots of tourists here, and a slew of very
pesky vendors on every street selling guide service, sight-
seeing tours, taxi service and every kind of trinket
imaginable. We ask our driver if we can stop for a beer
somewhere but he speaks so little English that I'm not sure
he understands and we go right through town down to Phu
Bai and the airport. When we get to the airport he rushes
us up to the toilets so we're thinking that he misinterpreted
our desires. But relief comes in many forms and that
certainly is one.

Like a lot of the airports here, when our flight is called we
all get on a bus and ride about 20 seconds, maybe less, out
to the airplane, debark from the bus and embark onto the
plane. Mike on my right by the window and Liz, a young
Vietnamese American on my left. Liz goes to school in
Toronto. Her parents are *Viet-Kieu* and own a restaurant in
Saigon. She is here visiting. I ask her about the restaurant
and she tells me it is a very high class place with
exceptionally good food in the Hue tradition. Mike and I
promise to eat there, and she gives us the name and
address.

Viet Kieu translates literally as overseas Vietnamese or
foreign Vietnamese. My understanding is that this term is
most commonly used to describe Vietnamese who left the
country and have returned for either visitation or relocation
purposes. They are treated somewhat differently and not
altogether welcomed back with opened arms by the current
government. They face many obstacles, both socially and

politically. Until just recently for instance, they were not allowed to own homes.

Chapter 14
Ho chi Minh City

We land in HCM City and grab a taxi to take us downtown to the Rex Hotel. It is 5 o'clock and rush hour. Driving through HCMC during rush hour traffic is quite an experience, that's for sure. A hundred motorcycles and a smattering of cars all in the middle of the same intersection at the same time with no stop sign or traffic light makes for slow progress, but there is no road rage, no yelling or screaming or fist waving. Just constsnt weaving back and forth trying to get to the other side. Eventually, everyone does. Once at the hotel, we check into our room, clean ourselves up and head to the open air Rooftop Garden Bar for dinner, the same bar where Mike and John played the trick on me last year. Both of us order racks of lamb and it is very good. Mike gets beer, I order a bottle of wine. After dinner we move over to a table on the rail, over looking downtown Saigon. It's quite a sight. Not as dramatic as the view from the top of the Majestic which sits on the Saigon River, but this is the Rex and with the historical context, it doesn't get much better. By 9 or 9:30 the place is pretty packed. There is a large private party for some Brits over on one side with traditional Vietnamese dancers and instruments. I move in as close as possible for some pictures and get kicked out twice. I figure I can't push my luck any more.

On the main section where we are, the band begins to play and they are really hot, playing a Jamaican Rock kind of beat. The place is packed now and I can't help myself, I get up and ask a stranger to dance. She says no but the young woman next to her needs to dance too and we go out and have fun with the music. I am barefooted because my legs and feet are still way too swollen to get my shoes on but I don't care. Alcohol is adequate anesthesia. And besides, dancing is dancing the world 'round and I am a dancing fool. Music makes my feet move. I'm quite sure I will dance in my grave.

After dancing myself out, or at least until my swollen feet can't take it anymore, Mike and I sip our beer and wine until the wee hours and downtown Saigon closing time. I go to bed thinking that I am once again in Saigon where so many people would love to be and yet what I really want is to be back in the smaller city of Dong Ha with the Nguyens and the less sophisticated Vietnamese of the central coast and highlands. There is where I feel more comfortable, more connected.

29 March, Saturday

This is our only full day here in HCMCity. We are both up about 6:30 and we get down to breakfast soon after. I have been having some bad GI problems for the past day or two and don't know what to attribute it to. This morning my feet are really swollen, I have a wicked headache and feel out of sorts. I am hoping it's just a hangover and will soon pass. The only thing I can wear on my feet are flip flops.

We kind of wander around for an hour or so and decide to go back to the Rooftop for a beer. It's about 10am. There is a trio of Caucasian looking women drinking beer and sitting at a table along the rail overlooking downtown, so we sit at the table next to them. As soon as we get our beers we start talking to them and by the second or third sentence, Mike asks if we can come over and sit with them. They are tentative but reluctantly agree. They introduce themselves as Laura, Lasca and Yvonne, all from San Fransisco. Laura and Lasca are lawyers and it seems obvious to me that they are a couple. I get the sense that

Yvonne is a paralegal, as is my wife Colette. The three women are all close friends and are here in Vietnam for a week or two on holiday. They are in high spirits, have quick smiles and it is easy to see that these are good people.

It turns out that we have a great conversation about all sorts of stuff, domestic and foreign, and we stay and talk until about 2pm when they tell us they have to move on to other things. Of course we invite them back for tonight's party on the rooftop. I'm thinking that we will probably not get to enjoy their company again but I'm happy to have had some great conversation for a short while.

The Rex is a large hotel with many levels and many small "roof top" pools, bars and gardens. Mike and I wander around, trying to find some quiet, out of the way garden that has a bar and find a nice place next to a pool and delightfully indulge in people watching and a cool drink. About 4:30 we go back to the room to clean up and get ready to go out to Liz's parents' fancy restaurant.

It's now 5:30 pm local time. I am as dressed up as I can possibly be in my Ex-Officio tropical pants and shirt, and flip flops for my swollen feet since they will fit into nothing else. Mike is in his finest T-shirt and jeans. We hire a cab to take us to Thans's Restaurant and find that it is at the very end of a long alley of restaurants. The moment we walk in it becomes obvious that this really is a high class place. I'm impressed. One wall is lined with bottles of wine, and for a change; they look like the real things. We are approached by a waiter and I ask if the owners are on the premises because I would like to talk with them. Translation is not very good and the waiter leaves and about 5 minutes later comes back with another employee who speaks some English. I again ask for the owner and he somewhat defensively asks why I need to talk with the owner. I tell him about meeting Liz on the plane and that we are happy and excited to be at their restaurant. He excuses himself and returns a few minutes later with a phone, which he hands to me. On the other end is Liz. She is just profusely appreciative of our patronage and explains that her parents cannot be there tonight but tells me that the restaurant will give us a free desert. The wait staff is now a bit more attentive.

Mike and I decide that we are going to eat whatever is the specialty of the house. We have a very nice dinner of lobster and stuffed prawns but the bill, including wine comes to $100 U.S. Oh well, I have spent more money on lesser things and I am satisfied that we have had fine Vietnamese cuisine.

Right now, all I want to do is get back up on the roof top at the Rex and mentally prepare for heading back to America. I am sad and happy. Once again, I don't want to leave but I am missing home, friends, Colette and my boys. I am really feeling like crap and I mostly just want to sit quietly with Mike and enjoy my last night in Vietnam. I cannot imagine getting the chance to come back here, but one can never tell and sick or not, I want to breath in every last drop of this city.

We get into the elevator at the Rex, head up to the roof top, find a table along the rail overlooking downtown and Mike and I are alone again 12 floors above SaiGon. We sip our drinks until the bar won't serve us any more, about 2 am. Other than the wait staff, we are the only ones left. Most of the staff is crowded around a small TV watching a soccer match.
Reluctantly, we drag ourselves up to our room and hit the sack. We will leave for the airport and our respective homes tomorrow late morning.

Chapter 15
Seattle Anxiety

Sunday, 30 March

We both get up fairly early and get most of our packing done quickly. We grab another great breakfast on the rooftop after which I take a nice walk and head over to the Banh Ton market where I get lots of pictures and buy a Vietnamese military style cover and two very red T shirts with the bright yellow Vietnamese star in the center.
By 10:30, Mike and I have our packs and are once again at the Rooftop Garden for a parting beer. Soon, we are off in a cab for Tan Son Nhot Airport and our respective journeys home. We talk a bit about some planning for bringing another group over and about our homes and what awaits us. I will check my pack, but my carry on is heavy with pepper, tamarind and coffee as well as other stuff. I don't particularly want to lug this stuff around wearing just flip flops but I still can't get my feet into my shoes. My GI problems are not going away and neither is the incredibly intense headache I have. Today I am feeling very weak and out of sorts. The last time I felt this bad was 1969 when I had the Hong Kong flu. I certainly don't relish the long trip back feeling like this, but I'm hoping a good night's sleep will cure my ills.

The flights from Saigon to Taipei and from there to Seattle are very lonely. Two trips over in the past year and my heart weighs heavy. DaNang, the Nguyens, and all of Vietnam, has touched me more deeply than I would have ever guessed. I want so much to be back at home with my wife and boys, but I am beginning to have this creeping sense of belonging to two places. For the past 40 plus years Vietnam has been a part of me that I tried in myriad ways to escape, nearly killing myself in the process. Now I find that it is an integral part of me, stuck to me like glue, a part that I am learning to embrace and desire. It is a strange dichotomy of pain and healing, like Yin and Yang, but an ever moving and changing perception of the place of pain becoming the salve of healing. There is an addicting quality to it all.

Perhaps there are many elements involved in my feelings. The making of new friends; not having deadlines or stress from professional responsibilities like I do back home; having unusual experiences, some of which are physically demanding and dangerous, all these create special bonds and memories. I am a sucker for that kind of excitement and for new adventures. Perhaps time in DaNang and trips into the jungle would eventually become routine. For right now however, I am saddened to say good bye to this beautiful country and these warm and caring people. I am trying to feel good about leaving.

When we arrived in Seattle, we had to clear customs in order to leave the airport or connect to another flight. That meant that all luggage had to be taken off the plane, picked up and we had to sort of reenter the airport through a customs gate. There were several stops where we were asked what we were bringing into the country. Also, while waiting at the carousel for our luggage, there were customs officers walking around, randomly asking for passports and custom declarations of what we were bringing or not bringing into the country. I had indicated on my declaration that I had coffee beans and pepper, but did not put down the Tamarind, fearing they would take it. At about the 3rd stop, before I got to the carousel, I was nervous enough that I decided to mention the Tamarind and the guy didn't even blink. No problem. They are looking for meat, dairy and other agricultural products. When I finally got my bag, I slung it over my shoulder and headed for the last customs stop before the flight to Detroit. Just then a young customs officer asks to see my declaration card and asks about my trip. I give him a thumbnail description and also proudly mention to him that I have dirt from the top of Hill 362 that I will be handing out to my Marine Corps mates at our next reunion. At the mention of the dirt he closes his eyes and puts his head down and says, "Sir, you can't bring dirt from another country into our country." A shiver runs right up my back and I say to him, "Please officer, don't take this dirt from me. It has more meaning than I could possibly explain." He looked at me for a few seconds and said that what I did over there was very special and that I should stuff the dirt deep into my bag and when I get to the last customs check, I shouldn't mention that I have it. Wow. I truly wish I had gotten that officer's name. He deserves a thank you card. And a Christmas present.

I had hoped to see John at the Seattle airport since he lives in the area, but he could not make it. We talked a bit on the phone and I could tell he had wanted so much to be with us. I hope he knows how much that feeling was mutual. As John and I talk, I am sitting in a largely empty terminal waiting for my flight to Detroit thinking that the third part of this story would be to take the "Ten Good Men" back to the site of the memorial so that they, too, could share in the closure. Again I feel lonely and home sick. The feelings exacerbated by whatever illness this is that has a hold of me. And again, it is a desire for two places.

Chapter 16

Finally home and I have to go back to work the very next day. Kind of like taking a G-force turn. Like nothing ever happened. Both Mike and I are settling in, however. He on Guam, me here in Detroit. Some sort of normalcy I suppose, but already I feel like I am waiting. Just tapping my fingers and toes and waiting. Waiting to return to Vietnam. There is a growing sense of an incomplete job.

I want to say again here that none of this could have happened without the incredible amount of research and work that Ngoc and Phong did, and of course Thach, the local guide who I took to calling The Rock Lady because she is so solid and determined. We've made deep and lasting friendships. All of them are determined and gritty guides, not afraid to take on any mission to any locale, regardless of hazards. Their work was spectacular. They epitomize the perseverance and hard work that characterizes the Vietnamese people.

This trip took much more out of me than last year. I am quite sure the same goes for Mike. I had places on my body that were sore for many weeks. I was diagnosed with Leptospirosis, a bacterial disease I must have picked up in the swampy waters of the stream bed, soon after I got home, but with proper medication I was feeling well soon enough. But bruises, diseases and leeches aside, there is a deep satisfaction with this accomplishment. After nearly 3 years of planning, 2 trips and almost 4 weeks of in-country prep work and slogging through jungle mountain terrain, I think the main work is now completed. Future visits to this place will be to a spot found and marked, a place for prayer, remembrance and healing.

Phong, Mike, doc, Linh (Kim), Ngoc
March 27, 2009
Dong Ha, Vietnam

A Trip Forward into the Past
Part 3

Ho Chi Minh and Disappointment

In front of the Ho Chi Minh Mausoleum, HaNoi
Sarge, Stan, doc, Mike, Gary, John, Don, Dick, Tom

May, 2013

After returning home from my last trip to Hill 362, I slowly began to feel as if we had not achieved complete closure. Well, we will never have *complete* closure. The Vietnam War, our experiences during that war and most specifically Operation Hastings and our epic battle on that little hill top is indelibly printed onto all of us who experienced those times. Because of that, we will never be the same again. The innocence we lost can never be recovered. I remember my sister telling me one night recently about her impression of me when I came home from the war: She had said to herself: "This is not the brother I remember, not the brother I grew up with." But closure, even partial closure, often times comes in slow, small steps that take years to achieve. So, three years after placing our memorial on that hill top, I began calling the original group of 10 and asking if they felt they had enough closure to satisfy themselves. To a man, they responded that they did not. Soon enough, I began planning yet another trip back to those mountains in hopes that those other Marines could bury some ghosts of their own.

I will not describe in detail all of our travels on this last trip. Rather, I will just include the few letters home that I wrote while we were there. I hope you find them not only enjoyable but enlightening as well.

HaNoi

May 7, 2013

There are no rules when it comes to driving here in Vietnam. Well, there are rules, but it seems like no one obeys them. HaNoi is a city of 7.5 million people and 3.5 million motorbikes. It's nearly impossible to walk on many of the sidewalks because there are just too many motorbikes parked on them so nearly everyone walks in the street, at least here in the Old Town section. The street, of course, is also filled with motorized bikes. They come at you on both sides of the street no matter which way you are headed and they weave in and out, left and right getting around a cacophony of sounds from vendors, sight seers, travelers, local workers and inhabitants sitting outside on sidewalk cafes and the like. In the Old Town section this organized chaos is everywhere.

So many of the motorbikes are small scooter types. The government applies exorbitant taxes to motors larger than 175cc so there are few cars and large bikes. Off of the main thoroughfares there are some intersections with red lights, but not many, and there are some intersections with roundabouts but again, not many. Getting across an intersection, whether on foot, on motorbike or in a car is a study in physics and daredevilry. You pick out the path you want to travel and you watch for anyone who looks like they are going to intersect that path at a moment that will impede your travel, at which point you either pick another path or you slow down to prevent fender bender incidents. There is no waiting for red/green lights because no one ever fully stops, so it is a constant sea of right, left, lurching, slowing movements that I'm sure could be put to music. Lots of beeping horns but no one gets angry and no one appears to be in a hurry.

I'm so very glad to be here again. While this is my first visit to the city of HaNoi, the Asian culture of the southeast coast is much the same north to south. Dialect is different as you travel from one direction to the other and there are subtle cuisine differences, but despite 53 different cultural and distinct tribal genealogies, the people look the same and behave the same. They are kind, generous and incredibly industrious.

We will head to HaLong Bay tomorrow, then down to the Phong Nha caves. Those will be vacation type visits before we begin the trek west, into the jungle and our hill. I cannot express how happy I am that these guys are finally going to get to the top of Hill 362. Those that we don't think can make the climb physically will take a 4-wheel drive truck almost right up to the base of the hill. They can all make it from there, I'm sure. The truck ride will be brutal. It's going to toss them around like popcorn but they are going to get there. Mike and I have promised all of them that. Each of them deserves the opportunity to bury some of the ghosts we have carried all these years.

Much love to you all,
Be well,

doug

Best Laid Plans and Depressing News

May 13, 2013

Might as well get the bad news out of the way. I did not make it to the hill this time. I didn't even get close. In fact, while the rest of the guys took off from HaNoi to DongHoi, the Phong Nha Caves, DongHa and our hill top, Major Carey and I stayed in HaNoi because one of our party developed a serious case of kidney stones and had emergency surgery at The French Hospital of HaNoi.

Several days previous, Sarge told me he was having some discomfort on both sides of his abdomen. His description of the pain was very vague and it was sounding to me like muscle or skeletal pain. I did ask and he responded positively about past history of kidney stones, but still, his pain description wasn't making sense to me and he denied that it felt like his past kidney stone experience. However, on Friday evening he knocked on my door and said he could no longer take the pain. His skin color and the look on his face made it obvious that he was in need of more help than I could offer. It was at that time that he finally admitted that his urine output had decreased to almost nothing and that this was feeling like a "stone."

The hospital experience in HaNoi was nothing short of remarkable. After walking unannounced into the hospital lobby and talking with the desk clerk, he was in a hospital bed within 2 minutes and seen by a ER physician within the next 3 minutes. When the physician asked about our circumstances, I explained who we were and what we were doing in Vietnam. He said to me, and I quote: "If he is American War veteran, he gets top priority, right now."
You could have knocked me over with a feather. This was about 10pm on Friday evening. He had a CT scan in less

than 30 minutes after the examination. The scan showed that he had multiple stones, bilaterally, and one in each ureter blocking the path of the urine to the bladder as well as stones in the bladder itself. His right kidney was swollen considerably, his left appeared undersized and there was some sort of damage (stricture) of the left ureter. He had emergency surgery the next morning (Saturday) by the chief of the department of Urology. The surgeon removed 7, yes, seven stones and placed (double J) stents into each ureter.

For perspective, in December, 1972, the United States military dropped 20,000 tons of bombs onto HaNoi in a single operation that lasted over 11 days. Almost 2,000 tons a day. Known officially as Linebacker 2, many in the U.S. called it The Christmas Bombing. Today, an American US Marine Corps veteran of that war against them gets "top priority" in a HaNoi hospital. I am truly humbled by their compassion and I began to realize that this is where their strength comes from: Compassion not strictly for themselves but for humanity; humble servants of a dedication that extends beyond the self and makes them willing and able to cross any bridge, endure any hardship.

In spite of Sarge's protests and telling me how great he was feeling after the surgery, I had the unfortunate position to decide that he could not continue on with us. He was discharged on Sunday and I got him a flight from HaNoi back to Utah on Monday. He arrived home, safe and sound.

Tuesday, Mike and I rejoined the tour in DaNang and were immediately confronted with shocking and depressing news. As the group made their way onto the top of the hill where I planted the memorials in 2009, a large part of the forest had been harvested for pulp wood and they were much better able to determine the exact position. What they discovered was that they were not on Hill 362. They were able to see, quite clearly, one set of hills to the west, our intended goal. They had their picture taken on the west slope of the hill Mike and I had found, with 362 in the background. As I looked at that picture, I knew there could be no doubt; I had planted those stones on the wrong hill. This was deeply disturbing, especially for me. Not only did I miss the opportunity to reunite with all the local DongHa people that helped me on my previous quest, I also erred in my topography on that prior arduous adventure. Now, we did not have the time or resources to go further and do more searching to find a way up the newfound 362. As a result, 6 years of planning and several trips into the mountains and we still have not conquered our hill top. I cannot express how heavy my heart is and how badly I feel for all of these guys. The feelings of elation I had have now become unfounded. What to do.

Be well,
doug

LongPhu Villages

May 20, 2013

After Operation Hastings and the battle on Hill 362, India Company was sent to guard two small villages just outside of ChuLai, south of TamKy. We needed time to recover and refill our ranks. The villages, called LongPhu 1 and LongPhu 2, were preparing to harvest their rice and manioc crops and we were assigned security for them so that the VietCong did not take the crops. Also, we provided medical and dental services for the village inhabitants. We stayed there for 3 straight months. We brought them toys, candy, balloons and a lot of soap. We vaccinated a lot of people, treated their illnesses and generally tried to improve their quality of life. We made friends with the people and for all of these 47 years in between, continue to think of them, wondering how they fared after we left them and just what exactly they thought of us.

It was Gary Crowell's idea to petition the company and see how many pictures the guys have of those two villages from 1966-67. He put a fantastic photo album together and we arranged to stay in the ChuLai area for 4 full days so that we could walk through those villages, showing our pictures, hoping upon hope that someone would recognize a picture and that would lead to another and another. Realistically, we expected perhaps 2 or 3 people who might recognize a picture and remember us. What we got was a gold mine. As word spread that there were Americans in the village showing photographs, people began to congregate. A 60 year old woman saw a very clear close up of herself from the fall of 1966 and the look on her face and the smile she gave us was worth the price of admission. She recognized several people and took us to their houses. Those people recognized more people and soon all of these older village elders are talking about the old days and where the U.S Marines were and where the VC were and remembering the times we spent there. We met the old man who was the village chief in 1967. We found the foundation remains of the old school building which was a marker of sorts for us. And we found people who opened their homes to us on a moment's notice, making sure we all had chairs to sit in, had cool tea to drink and that we were comfortable. We found an elderly blind woman, 82, who was the wife of an ARVN (Army of the Republic of Vietnam - South Vietnam) who also provided protection not only for the villages but for us Marines as well. And we met his son and daughter in law. He was so well liked by everyone on both sides of the war that after it he was not sent to re-education camp but instead allowed to stay at home, although closely watched. A rare occurrence, to be sure.

As I mentioned before, part of the reason we did this people search this time is because we are really curious to know how the people felt about us and if they thought we actually did provide them with real help. Did they like us? Were we a disrupting entity at the time? Do they think as kindly of us as we do of them? Of course it seems rude to just approach someone you haven't seen in nearly 50 years, where you were the foreigner and perhaps seen as an invader and just straight out ask, "Did you like us? Did we provide acceptable, tangible help? Did you want us there?" As the days went on, no one volunteered answers to these unasked questions, but we got the feeling more and more that there was a sense of fond memories on the part of the villagers, until we found one last guy who recognized a picture of himself at the age of 11, holding his baby sister in his arms. He lived on the outskirts of LongPhu 2. After looking at the pictures and telling us all he knew about the people in them he said to us that everyone in these villages are better off because of our input in their lives, that everyone has fond memories of us and that very few of the people who lived there in late 1966 and early 1967 ever forgot our attempts at helping them have happier and healthier lives. He said the next time we come back he would invite us to stay in his house for as long as we would like. And then he said, "On behalf of every one, I want to thank you for what you did for us." As we walked along the narrow path leading away from his humble home that late afternoon, I doubt that I was the only one to have tears in my eyes.

Mission accomplished.

Be well,
doug

Final Thoughts

May 23

The more time you spend with people, the more you get to know them. There are first impressions and there are significant moments that create lasting memories and after a while, you begin to see deeper into what a person or a culture is like.

The first time I went back to Vietnam after the war, I was a little nervous. I didn't know what the people would be like or how they would treat us. It was over 40 years since I had been here and there were 10 of us old, battle hardened and weary U.S. Marines. And I certainly didn't know what my reaction would be when I went to my most significant battle site, the site that haunted me all of my life. So, yeah, I was a little nervous. I found so much more than I expected. I found a country that is geographically beautiful. I think that's an understatement. It's an incredible place. It has some of the largest and deepest caves on the planet. HaLong Bay on the north end of the Haiphong bay area has these huge limestone monoliths sticking up out of the water all over the place, some of them with great caves, some with colonies of monkeys. The area around SaPa in the northwest has the most picturesque farmland I have ever seen with rows and rows of steeply terraced rice fields as well as the tallest mountain in the entire Indochina region. The Mekong Delta in the south was caused by the silt deposit of the Mekong River, which begins in Tibet and runs through China and Burma (Myanmar), Thailand, Cambodia, Laos and Vietnam and might have the richest soil on earth and most certainly grows some of the richest rice and a large percentage of the rice on earth. The jungles still have ancient forests and still grow some of the most sought after wood in the world. Mountains of marble rise up from the sandy beaches along the mid coast. Not large mountains, and no foot hills, they just jut up out of the sand not 1/4 mile off the ocean shore, the beach that the Americans used to call China Beach. And I just can't even begin to describe the incredible food, particularly the seafood of this coastal country; so elegantly simple and deeply flavored. Not to mention that I could eat BBQ squid every day of my life.

And the people.........how could this history create such quiet, caring, giving and industrious people after more than 100 years of war defending their lands? Through all of their wars they never lost touch with their past, their culture. Each family is strongly and daily connected not only to all of the relatives that are alive, but all of those who went before them as well as all of those that have not yet been born. They are the conscious and mindful connection from the past to the future. The Vietnamese are fiercely independent and entrepreneurial, almost to a fault. It is the spirit of the family that keeps them together. Most Vietnamese are not interested in making a million dollars. Well, maybe some are, and, of course, there is corruption as there is in any government, but for the most part, the average Vietnamese just wants to make enough to get along and not have any one regulate them or tell them what to do, and I mean no one. They are persistent in that right down to every vendor on the street who has only a few coconuts to sell. Those street vendors that are everywhere, in every city. I suggest that you ask the French, Japanese, Chinese, Cambodian, Russian and American governments how persistent the Vietnamese are in wanting to be left alone.

After the Korean War, Vietnam dominated the political landscape for much of the 50's, 60's and 70's. Yes, there was the Cold War and the Cuban Missile crisis and Sino-

Soviet tensions, but Vietnam held the attention of the major players on the planet for a very long time and changed many of the geopolitical relations significantly.

And Ho Chi Minh, the father of Vietnam, who, from very humble beginnings wanted nothing more than a truly independent nation, was always at the center of it. He is "Uncle Ho" to all of the people here, and he always will be. And I sang Happy Birthday to him on the 19th of May and I toasted to him and I visited him at his grave site and I admire and respect him for all that he did for his country. And if you don't believe that he was a great man, a larger than life man, then you don't know his history. And I say all of that as a proud and patriotic United States Marine Corps FMF Corpsman.

Belonging to two places

When I started writing this note, all I wanted to do was make a note to myself about how independent the Vietnamese are. This is a special place for me. It provides sustenance to my heart and soul and part of me will always want to be here. I have found a place that has made me love it. I found a people that I want to embrace. I have found comfort here, I have found peace and I have found what I did not know I was looking for: I found acceptance. So strange that the one thing that I thought would be forever out of my reach, acceptance, I would find in the place farthest away from where I was looking so desperately. The innocence that I lost so long ago, the part of my soul that was torn away from me, lives in all of the people here, all of the villages. It lives in their culture, in their art, on the streets, in their markets and in their homes. My blood is in the soil of their country. I know that I cannot bring it home with me. It belongs here and I am now OK with that. I know they will keep it well for me. I know they will give it the same respect and reverence they give all things spiritual. I will always be able to reconnect with that part of my soul, but only here, only here. It needs to stay here. How could it possibly be otherwise?

Prior to the trip, during my planning, I thought that once we were done with our trips to DaNang, ChuLai and trying to find our hill, I wanted to have something special for the guys on our last couple of days in the country. I thought a great idea was to take them to the very beach where we made our first landing in Vietnam with the hostile intent of waging war. That place would be what in 1966 we called Red Beach, on *Xuan Dai* bay along the south central coast. We were young, very well trained and itching for a fight. Few of us knew the realities of war back then. But "Red Beach" and our very first operation are a place and time we will all remember.

I arranged to have a large banner made proclaiming the site as, "Red Beach Bar and Grill," and indicating our first landing date (0635 Hrs 18 June, 1966) as well as our final departure date, figuring that this would finally be our very last trip to this country. I also arranged to have a chef come out to the beach and cook lobster, shrimp, crabs and chicken and set up tables, umbrellas and coolers full of cold beer. It was a great day. We had the beach almost entirely to ourselves and we spent 6 hours there eating, talking, reminiscing and walking along the beach before we left.

That night, our last night before heading back to HaNoi and our flights home, we stayed at a 5-star luxury resort and spa nearby. It would have been the perfect ending had we not discovered the topographical error of the 2009 trip and the resulting misplaced memorials. So, now we are left with mulling over the possibility of having to try yet again. Are we doomed to failure? Are the spirits telling us not to

come? Not to tread on the hallowed ground of that hill top?
Not to unearth the blood spilled there? Is this India
Company's "mission that will not end?" Soon, it will be 50
years from the date of that engagement. It still feels like
yesterday.

Dick, Stan, Doc, Mike, Gary, John, Don, Tom

They say that home is where the heart is and today I am at the airport waiting for the plane to take me to America. I'm really happy to come back to the United States and so very sad to leave here. This place, the source of so much of my pain for so many years, is now my salve, and no matter which direction I am traveling, toward Vietnam or toward the U.S.A., I know I am headed toward my heart, I am headed home.

Be well,
Doug

In front of Hill 362 May, 2013

Showing the India Company flag we had with us in 1966,
kept by John Olsen, and the men who gave their lives
embroidered on upper left corner

Also available at Amazon.com

52051472R00088

Made in the USA
San Bernardino, CA
09 August 2017